"Anybody in *any* organization who has *any* responsibility must read this book."

—Warren Bennis, Distinguished Professor of Business,
University of Southern California and author of *On Becoming a Leader*

"Provocative and unique . . . *The Right Fight* illustrates how a healthy dose of tension energized some of the world's most respected companies. It worked at Campbell."

—Douglas R. Conant,
President and CEO, Campbell Soup Company

"Managing tension and conflicting ideas is but part of the equation. Using them to steer the organization toward success is the other part, which is often overlooked. In *The Right Fight*, Saj-nicole Joni and Damon Beyer show us how to use conflict the right way!"

—Marshall Goldsmith is the *New York Times* bestselling author of *Succession: Are You Ready?* and *What Got You Here Won't Get You There*

"Tensions are the road to competitiveness, while consensus often leads to mediocrity. Saj-nicole, the nicest person on earth got it right—encouraging the right fight is the hallmark of true leadership. Great ideas are born from competition, and thrive when subjected to survival of the fittest."

—Rolf Classon, Chairman,
Hill-Rom, and former CEO, Bayer Healthcare

"If you care about how well organizations work, you need to buy this book, get out a highlighter, and mark up the pages. It will change the way you think about teams and how they're run. And it will raise your collective performance and sense of satisfaction."

—Bridgette Heller, Global President,
Johnson and Johnson Consumer Companies

"The authors have absolutely nailed one of the critical unspoken tools in the leadership tool kit. The book helped me reflect on the right and wrong fights of the past and begin planning my next one!"
—Gaurdie E. Banister Jr.,
President and CEO, Aera Energy LLC

"If you're a leader at any level, *The Right Fight* will inspire you to embrace organizational tensions, and in so doing, release the energies needed to solve your most complex problems. This is one of the most practical business books I've read and I recommend it highly."
—Jacqueline Novogratz,
founder and CEO, Acumen Fund, and author, *The Blue Sweater*

"The wisdom runs deep and the stories jump off the page. Joni and Beyer show us why alignment is not enough. Fighting the right fights right can be the difference between survival and extinction. This book should be at the top of any leader's reading list."
—Doug Stone, coauthor of the *New York Times* bestseller
Difficult Conversations: *How to Discuss What Matters Most*

"*The Right Fight* pokes a sharp stick at management complacency and empowers leaders to drive organizations to peak performance."
—Carter McClelland, Chairman, Union Square Advisors

"If you want to have impact you must read this book. Taking on the seemingly impossible becomes very real when you pick the right fights along the way—everything is within reach with this approach"
—Maria Eitel, President of the Nike Foundation

"For managers facing the real-life challenge of getting teams to be effective day in and day out, *The Right Fight* offers new insight and practical ways to make agreement productive."
—Dan Ciampa, CEO advisor and author of
Taking Advice: How Leaders Get Good Counsel and Use it Wisely

The
RIGHT
FIGHT

ALSO BY SAJ-NICOLE JONI

The Third Opinion

The
RIGHT
FIGHT

How Great Leaders Use Healthy
Conflict to Drive Performance,
Innovation, and Value

SAJ-NICOLE JONI
and DAMON BEYER

HARPER
BUSINESS

An Imprint of HarperCollins*Publishers*
www.harpercollins.com

HarperCollins books may be purchased for educational, business, or sales promotional use. For information, please write: Special Markets Department, HarperCollins Publishers, 10 East 53rd Street, New York, NY 10022.

FIRST EDITION

Designed by Cassandra J. Pappas

Library of Congress Cataloging-in-Publication Data
Joni, Saj-nicole A.
The right fight : how great leaders use healthy conflict to drive performance, innovation, and value / Saj-nicole Joni and Damon Beyer.—1st ed.
    p. cm.
Includes bibliographical references.
ISBN 978-0-06-171716-1
1. Leadership. I. Beyer, Damon. II. Title.
HD57.7.J664 2010
658.4'092—dc22
                                                        2009018885

10 11 12 13 14   OV/RRD   10 9 8 7 6 5 4 3 2 1

To the memory of Patricia Zander (1942–2008),
and her courageous fight for life, music,
love, and human possibility.

—SNJ

To my wife, Cindy, for her unfailing love,
support, brilliance, and amazing sense of humor.

—DMB

CONTENTS

Contents

INTRODUCTION

I

AS HUMANS, WE know we have to change. It is our condition, part of our DNA. We are at our best when we meet change head on. But how do we function when the implications are bewildering, the pace accelerates relentlessly, and the direction seems dangerous? Today these questions play out on a global scale.

This book is about the answer: leadership that creates breakthrough performance, meaningful innovation, and lasting value, leadership that discerns the difference between real progress and the shortsighted thinking that seems good for a while but then leads people right off the edge of a cliff.

The prospect of change always brings up tough questions. How do we move forward with confidence that we're heading in the right direction? How do we ensure that we are addressing everyone's critical needs? What checks and balances do we need to avoid disaster?

For most people who study and write about leadership,

the answer to all of these questions has been found in the concept of *alignment*. Create enough alignment around a common purpose and you can solve even the most difficult challenges. But when we need to innovate on a grand scale, or to change essential aspects of an organization or a group, agreement is only half the answer.

In this book we argue that the path forward requires a healthy dose of *dissent* as well. Our most important ideas need to be refined in the fire of debate. It is a leader's job to work within the debate to find the best way forward. No single perspective holds all the answers. Any single idea taken too far can become destructive.

What does this mean for you? We have spent the last decade working across the globe with leaders at all levels who by circumstance or by dint of personality have embraced managing dissent as a critical aspect of their leadership. We have seen firsthand the power of "right fights" to create breakthrough performance, deliver lasting innovation, and groom the next generation of leaders. Our goal is to make these insights, and the skills that go along with them, widely available to leaders in all organizations at all levels.

We will take you from the rehearsal halls of Broadway to an impoverished village in India, from the executive suite of a major global company to the chaotic office of a small start-up, from a local school system to the White House, as we explore what all these diverse places have in common: a need to put productive tension to good use in the face of extraordinary challenges. In short, places just like your organization.

Tension is universal, and the need to manage it is deeply

human. Done well, right fights bring out the best of human capacity. Wrong fights—or right fights that never happen—can distort a noble purpose into a massive failure, with lots of innocent people getting hurt along the way. Right fights matter in the largest corporations, in small nonprofits, in governments, and in every organization in between. They matter in local communities and they matter on a global scale. They matter in times of growth and in times of recession.

What it really takes to lead people and organizations is this: if you want to succeed in an age of ever-increasing complexity you have to establish clear vision, set strategy, and build alignment. Then you need to systematically orchestrate *right fights—and fight them right.*

II

In spite of the fact that few of us feel we thrive on conflict, right fights benefit people and organizations in three ways:

1. **Right fights lower risk.** Effective systems of checks and balances always depend on vigorous dissent.
2. **Right fights create value.** They live at the heart of innovation, breakthrough, and real change.
3. **Right fights grow better leaders.** They are the surest way to develop the leadership skills and strategic thinking necessary for the twenty-first century.

You can learn to create healthy conflict and positive change by choosing the right fights. Of course, you have to be careful. You've probably seen right fights fought wrong that failed to produce results, and of course wrong fights, even if fought right, are worthless.

The challenge is to choose the right fights and fight them right.

In this book you will learn to do both. We provide three principles to help you figure out whether you are in a right fight. And we provide three more principles to show you how to fight the fights right. Along the way there are lots of examples to illustrate what we mean and to help you lead your teams and organizations successfully.

III
THE SIX RIGHT FIGHT PRINCIPLES

The first three Right Fight Principles will guide you in recognizing right fights. We have all worked in organizations that were destructively political. We have all watched otherwise rational people go to extreme lengths to sabotage their counterparts or to retaliate against colleagues who have offended or threatened them in some way. And we have all seen people fight dirty when they believe that straight shooting won't get the job done. The first three Right Fight Principles will help you in identifying and eliminating these destructive tensions.

First, make it worth fighting about: make it material. Fighting is hard even when you know it will bring out the best in people in the long run. So make the stakes big enough to motivate everyone and help everyone feel that the game is worth the candle.

Second, focus on creating the future. If you're arguing about the past, or rehashing power struggles, or apportioning blame, then you're not fighting the right fight. That's as close to an absolute rule as we can offer. Right fights are about the future, not the past.

Third, pursue a noble purpose. Make your fight about improving the lives of customers, for example, or changing the world for the better. Right fights connect people with a sense of purpose that goes beyond their own self-interest, unleashing profound collective abilities to create in ways they didn't think possible.

The last three Right Fight Principles guide you in fighting right fights right.

Fourth, make it sport, not war. Even though business fights are tough and can sometimes get ugly, good leaders establish themselves as referees to make sure that things don't get out of hand. There should be rules for the fight and the rules shouldn't change during the conflict. And opposing sides should be reasonably matched.

Fifth, structure formally, but work informally. Organizations have both formal and informal structures. Successful leaders structure right fights through the formal organization, exploiting imperfect alignment in the chain of command, measures, and incentives. But they make right fights work through the informal organization, the networks of personal and professional connections that are not on the org chart. It's there that you can forge powerful personal trust relationships, create coalitions, and help good ideas triumph in spite of the hierarchy.

And finally, turn pain into gain. Putting your people under tension isn't easy. But when the fights are the right ones and leaders manage them right, the struggle will energize people and stretch their skills. A hallmark of right fights is that when they are orchestrated well, everyone who participates benefits from the outcome—even the losers. It's the leader's job to make the gains explicit, especially at key moments when losers are coming to terms with their loss.

We hope this book will help you and your teams decide what's worth fighting about, so that when you do fight in your organization, you're fighting about the things that really matter. And we hope to show you how to conduct the fight with great skill, passion, and compassion. In the heat of battle you want to be sure that your conduct is guided by our simple, sturdy set of principles, so that you fight in ways that help people grow, develop respect for diverse views, and leave everyone whole— ready and energized to do battle again another day.

Part

ONE

ALIGNMENT
and TENSION *in*
ORGANIZATIONAL
LIFE

Alignment Is Not the Whole Answer

WE CAN HARDLY blame you for being skeptical.

If you're like most people in the business world, you've always been told by teachers, managers, colleagues, and business gurus that the single most important thing leaders have to get right is alignment.

To accomplish anything, the logic goes, employees must agree about the mission, strategy, and goals of an organization. Aligned employees are happy employees, and happy employees are productive employees.

Simple, right?

Well, in a word, no. What's going on here is that many people mistake the comfortable feeling that alignment brings for the real conditions necessary for optimal performance.

A well-aligned, smoothly functioning team can do a bad job well, or a job that shouldn't be done at all. The *Titanic*, by all accounts, was being run smoothly and well when it collided with an iceberg and sank. Because the team of sailors believed the ship was unsinkable, they ignored the initial signs of danger until it was too late. Ditto for Lehman Brothers, the investment bank that had one of the strongest cultures of teamwork and loyalty on Wall Street. They hit their own virtual iceberg and sank as well, almost taking the entire global economy with them in 2008. They, too, were aligned around their belief in an unsinkable ship and they were running it smoothly. Up until the moment that the water began pouring over the side and the ship began to tip into the ocean, the team was happy and satisfied with its lot.

Don't mistake what we're saying. Alignment is important. In fact, it's necessary. All those business books are right about that. You cannot win with a team that is badly aligned. The problem is, it's not sufficient. Achieving perfect or near-perfect alignment is not the end of the road. It's merely the beginning.

Let's take this a step further. Counter to conventional wisdom, the dirty little secret of leadership is that a leader's time is not always best spent trying to help his or her teams make nice and get along.

They don't tell you this in business school. Quite the contrary—business school, like everywhere else in the management world, is constantly harping on the value of teamwork and alignment.

Wait a minute, you object. I've worked for nice bosses and nasty bosses. The nice ones dole out the doughnuts or the compliments, and that makes your day. The nasty ones forget to praise, or throw out a cutting remark, and make the workplace poisonous.

4

What's wrong with being nice? What is the alternative?

Don't worry. We're not going to defend the nasty boss. And nice bosses the world over have our praise and thanks. What we are arguing is that in an environment where alignment is the only goal, alignment robs us of necessary dissent, of the checks and balances that mitigate risk, and of the tensions that create innovation and sustainable value.

TENSION IS PRODUCTIVE

At the heart of our argument is the counterintuitive, hard-to-swallow insight that a certain amount of healthy struggle is good for organizations and for individuals. Indeed, people and organizations perform optimally when they are under the right kinds and amounts of stress.

Tension is a good thing: for workers, for teams, and for organizations.

The concept of creative tension is not new. It's in the Bible, the Koran, the Bhagavad-Gita. It's been written about in the lives of artists, musicians, and scientists who have created breakthroughs that have changed the world. The U.S. Constitution depends on it, and we call on it as a motivating force every time we go out to vote. All successful treaties between nations—not to mention all successful relationships between people—work because it is not only possible but empowering to release in creative ways the energy inherent in tension.

It follows then that a key aspect of a leader's job is to create the right battles and to make sure they are fought right. Right fights unleash the creative, productive potential of teams, organizations, and communities. Right fights make for better possibilities. Right fights lead to better results.

With alignment and *properly managed tension*, organizations hit a sweet spot and start realizing their potential. With right fights, organizations can achieve breakthrough performance, real innovation, and leadership growth.

That's it. That's the central insight of this book. Right fights unleash the creative energy in people and organizations and allow them to thrive and achieve at their best possible levels. Right fights encourage diversity of views, they engender checks and balances, they inspire complex thinking and respect for difference. They are the cauldron in which new ideas are heated and mixed into the stew of new markets, processes, and products. They are the fuel of human innovation. And they provide a rich training ground for future leaders.

FINDING THE RIGHT LEVEL OF TENSION

Theresa Wellbourne, CEO of eePulse, has studied thousands of leaders, managers, and workers in businesses undergoing change over the past twenty years. She has found that the single greatest predictor of poor performance in a business group is when the employees are *happy*. That may surprise you. It seems counterintuitive. Isn't happiness what we're all aiming for?

A little detail helps here. Employees perform poorly when survey scores show they are *complacent* and thus not motivated to rock the boat and push the company in new directions.

The second greatest predictor of poor performance is when employees are *overwhelmed*—that is, when survey scores show low employee satisfaction and a large dose of dysfunctional fighting. The one thing both groups have in common is that they score very low on "energy." Complacent groups and overstressed groups both lack the necessary energy to perform at their best. Tension in the right measure creates the emotional energy people need to change.

Recent brain research points to the same thing. Dr. Paul Rosch, president of the American Institute of Stress, puts it simply: individual performance improves as stress increases— but only to a point. Past that point, performance declines precipitously, and if subjected to distress for extended periods of time, people get sick. Too many or too threatening fights trigger the amygdala and primitive, destructive "fight-or-flight" impulses flood the brain.

But within an acceptable range of competition and tension, more of the brain is firing, more pathways are stimulated, and more creative centers are engaged. In short, more of what makes each of us unique, creative, and passionate is available for use.

It's time to stop candy-coating our management teaching, training, and practice. It's time to stop pretending that teamwork is the be-all and end-all of organizational life. It's time to own up to the truth that the right balance of alignment and competition is what pushes individuals and groups to do their best. And once we do this, it's time to master the principles and skills to make this work.

LEADERS MUST SHOULDER NEW RESPONSIBILITY

This realization places great responsibility on your shoulders as a leader. It's simply not enough to create a peaceful and safe place to work. Your job is not done once you've explained the goal or shared the vision and gotten everyone to agree to it. That's only table stakes for competition in the twenty-first century.

The real game today is figuring out how to get a group of aligned team members, or an aligned organization, to produce its best results. What does it take to stay ahead of the marketplace, to serve the customer brilliantly, to dream up the next big thing? Where must we put in place checks and balances so that we don't collectively run off the cliff because we squelched some crucial dissent? Where must we counter the very real factor of human greed and systematically keep our passions in check to create sustainable futures, not disastrous bubbles?

From one organization to another, the answers will be different. Graphic designers work differently than structural engineers. A television newsroom requires different kinds of alignment and pressure than a state budget office. A university responds to different kinds of competition than an automaker's shop floor.

In the end, too, personal integrity will be at stake. We must look deep inside ourselves to our core beliefs, and create environments where people can collectively do more than they can do alone—with wisdom, humor, and a sense of honor for both peace and conflict. Tension brings out both the best and worst in workers and managers alike.

It's our goal to help you pursue the right balance of alignment and tension for your team, your division, your organization.

The good news is the skills are learnable. Although there is still a lot of art to this kind of leadership, the Right Fight Principles are clear. Applying them, you can easily distinguish a right fight from a wrong one, decide when to fight and when not to, and learn to turn the inevitable conflicts into productive performance.

PREPARE FOR THE RACE

Think of it like racing a sailboat. You have to prepare the mast, the sails, the boat itself, and the team. That's alignment. It's the key prerequisite because it ensures that once you get going, everything will be working together. But alignment by itself gets you nowhere until you have the tension of the wind in your sails. You're literally stuck at the dock.

And when you're actually at sea, the winds are going to change. The point of alignment is not to avoid the rough seas, but rather to be ready to exploit the tension created by the winds and the waves and the priorities of your crew—in the moment—in order to win the race.

So the job of the leader is to get the alignment right first, and then to find out how and when to inject the correct amount of tension into the organization to keep the sails taut, the line true, and the boat on an even keel. That's the only way in the end to win races in the marketplace.

You might say that our goal is to show leaders how to harness the power of the wind.

Let's get started. Let's get practical.

Let's look at some examples of right fights and wrong fights.

CASE STUDY: *Doug Conant Reinvigorates Campbell Soup Company*

- The CEO had to work on alignment first, tension second.
- Conant kept the focus squarely on the future—a right fight.
- A right fight is a process, not an event.

Be careful what you ask for. Doug Conant wanted a challenge when he stepped down as president of Nabisco and took the chief executive role at Campbell Soup Company in 2001. At the time Campbell was the poorest-performing major food company in the world.

Having experienced significant declines in performance across many measures, the company had fallen prey to an ill-advised effort to aggressively cut costs in hopes of restoring prosperity. Throughout the previous decade, management had systematically worked to lower the cost of its signature products, while at the same time raising prices. Finally, the situation became so challenging that they began to consider taking some of the chicken out of the chicken noodle soup. The once-revered American brand had lost its way.

Without a common view of what the organization was trying to accomplish, the leadership team was consumed with conflicting priorities and infighting over who was to blame for the mess they were in.

Conant knew that his immediate priorities were to manage the internal and external tensions the company was facing, then to fundamentally rebuild employee morale. It was no small task. A Gallup survey conducted in 2001 showed Campbell to have one of the poorest employee engagement cultures in the Fortune 500. Conant's first step was to remodel the organization to build alignment.

In his first ninety days, Conant set out to create a broad "tapestry of expectations" to rebuild trust with employees and make sure everyone understood where the company was headed. Working with his leadership team, he created a values statement, an "employees matter" promise, and a mission statement that ultimately focused and defined Campbell's purpose as "nourishing people's lives everywhere, every day."

Fixing the revenues and margins was important, but this noble purpose was Campbell's new true north. It made it clear that the company was going to win in the marketplace *and* in the workplace.

Although the team took six months to formally study pricing, innovation, and other fundamental causes of the decline, the team didn't fall into the easy temptation to lay blame and point fingers in their communications. Instead they focused on "the Campbell promise," stressing that the company had all the ingredients it needed to win. Conant was candid about the problems the company was facing, saying the company couldn't "talk its way out of a situation it had behaved its way into."

At the same time that he restored alignment, Conant knew he had to inject significant creative tension into the organization in order to make Campbell and its executives more energetic and effective. He started at the top. The organization was rearranged into a matrix, so the departure of any single leader would have less impact on the business, and a greater level of functional excellence would be brought to bear on every major decision.

To help with the transformation of the organization, Conant brought his colleague and confidant Robert Schiffner from Nabisco as CFO to restore the financial health and credibility of the company. Conant also hired a chief strategy officer to oversee the strategic reinvention of the company, a global chief information officer to oversee all IT, and a global chief supply officer to modernize Campbell's logistics and operations practices.

The new structure was designed to create productive debate between the various branches of the organization. Senior leaders were encouraged to produce and debate radical ideas to restore Campbell to its former glory. The immediate need was to restore the brand's reputation with customers and with Campbell employees in order to buy time to accomplish the long-term goal, a revival of product innovation and a return to a growing market presence.

Having completed the reorganization and renewed the company's vision, the people involved in the business had their immediate interests and goals aligned more productively. Now it was not just safe but desirable to encourage executives to produce thinking and plans that affected more than just their own departments. Conant took advantage of the tension between the plans and the debate over their relative priorities to create a series of right fights. He knew these right fights could restore the company's reputation and achieve the grand future vision he had for Campbell.

In the short term, as the facts about Campbell's fragile profile were uncovered, the investment community became nervous about a multiyear turnaround plan, and the stock price fell 30 percent. But the Campbell board of directors and the major shareholders stuck with Conant. Slowly but surely, his focus on the future began to work. Pricing came in-line. Product quality improved. The innovation pipeline became full again.

Margins were buttressed not by short-term slashing of product quality but by getting consumers to trade up to higher levels of product quality and new premium products. New product lines like Select Harvest ready-to-serve soups and whole grain Pepperidge Farm breads offered better nutritional credentials, and consumers viewed them as also offering improved quality and convenience.

The changes in the leadership team also produced better business results. Updated information systems allowed the team to refine promotional activities and improve margins. Innovations like gravity-fed merchandising systems won praise from consumers and retailers and reinforced the new image of a more convenient shopping experience.

To build trust with employees, Conant and his executive staff carefully trimmed the underperformers from the global leadership team. In all, 300 of the top 350 leaders left the company. Performance improved six years in a row.

By the end of 2008, Campbell was ranked in the top tier of food companies in financial performance and in the top quintile of companies in employee engagement, a proxy for employee morale. The company's mission and values statements continue to evolve, as does its frontline-created employee value proposition. The organization has evolved as well. Conant and his executive team have aligned the company even more closely with market trends and positioned Campbell to more effectively fight competitive battles.

There are many issues remaining that the company has yet to tackle. Concerns over volatile commodity prices and currency exposure in 2008 and 2009 created some temporary setbacks with investors. But it's striking that the new leadership team stayed the course. They tightened their cost structure and focused on shedding noncore businesses like Godiva Chocolates and on improving productivity, not reducing product quality. And they continue to emphasize margin improvement through innovation, not by risking and compromises to the company's restored reputation.

By balancing the inevitable pressure to produce quarterly earnings growth with the absolute passion to sustain the company and its brands in the long term, Conant and his team have created a truly lasting turnaround. In the series of right fights Conant has conducted since his arrival in the CEO's office, he has steadfastly maintained a constant focus on the long-term future of Campbell and its mission to nourish lives.

Herein lies one of the most important lessons of all. Fighting the right fight is at its core a discipline, not an event. To-day's battles move quickly and leaders must adapt or perish. Quickly moving battles require leaders always to be on the top of their game. But right fights are also useful in managing day-to-day issues that come up in the life of organizations.

ONE OF THE most difficult and important issues is one every organization faces at regular intervals if it survives: the question of succession. Succession, broadly speaking, is a right fight, even though it is to a great extent internally focused. The continuing existence of organizations depends, of course, on their ability to recruit new talent and to smoothly integrate that talent into the lineup without a stumble in terms of revenue, growth, or the like.

And yet it can be a perilous fight if it drains organizational attention and energy while it is going on. It is all too easy for the fight over succession to take up enormous amounts of managerial time and become an excuse for internal focus when an organization needs above all to keep doing what it is supposed to be doing in order to survive.

Let's look at how General Electric (GE) handled the search for Jack Welch's successor. It's important to understand that right fights are just as essential in healthy, successful companies like GE was in 1994 as they are in turnarounds like Campbell Soup. Whether you're focusing internally on succession or externally on sales, tensions help keep you clear about future performance and leadership. Alignment won't get you there by itself.

CASE STUDY: *Jack Welch Hires a Successor at GE*

- Good leaders make conscious choices to raise tensions to solve specific problems.
- Good leaders stay involved in the fights they raise to enforce the rules and to referee among combatants.
- It's not always fair; there are real winners and losers.
- In a right fight, everyone grows even if not everyone wins.

GE has long been regarded as one of the world's best companies. Beginning with its founding in 1878 by Thomas Edison, the company has grown steadily and reliably into the $173 billion in revenues giant that it is today, creating billions of dollars of shareholder value—and paying dividends—along the way.

From 2002 to 2007, the company managed to grow revenues at a compounded annual rate of 13 percent and earnings at 14 percent. Throughout the 1990s and the early part of the new millennium, the company was regularly praised for its management and its up-to-date business practices. From an early focus on centralization in the 1930s, GE transitioned to world-renowned strategic planning in the 1970s, and then became known for agility and global reach while Jack Welch was CEO in the 1980s and 1990s.

There have been fewer CEOs of GE during its 130-year history than there have been popes during the same time period. With all that history riding on GE's continued success, it's no wonder that when Welch set out to pick his successor in 1994, it was a four-year process just to narrow the field to three strong choices from twenty-three initial candidates.

CEOs of GE have about twenty years in the position, on average, and Welch figured that the first ten years were all about learning on the job. It takes that long to learn enough about the processes, methods, and levers of power to make a difference at an organization like GE. So he started out by looking at young leaders who could put their imprint on the company, as well as all the current business executives and senior corporate officers. But his primary focus was on the young leaders. No outside candidates were considered; GE believes that it has the best talent inside.

Welch's main goal, in addition to ensuring the continued dominance of the company, was to minimize internal politics while maximizing the odds of choosing the right successor so the company wouldn't stumble or lose focus while the high-stakes power struggle was going on. Welch hoped, at least initially, to create a three-man team with two vice chairs supporting the top person.

When Welch interviewed the three finalists in 1998—Bob Nardelli from power systems, Jim McNerney from aircraft engines, and Jeff Immelt from medical systems—he was impressed by how able each man was. It was going to be a difficult choice.

What he did to evaluate the three leaders was unusual. He looked for an appropriate, convincing test that would allow the three men to show their leadership skills without too much disruption to the company.

So Welch consciously launched a right fight. He started a

competition between the three men that focused on having each of them lead a major cross-company initiative, and train their own replacements, while at the same time continuing to run their own shows.

Inevitably, people from the executive suite down found subtle ways to play games and line up behind their choices. Overall, tensions heightened in the company. The amount of time spent in speculation, forming alliances, and angling for position up and down the line went up. But the contest allowed Welch to see how well each of the candidates would undertake a high-stakes managerial assignment under scrutiny.

Welch told each man that the one key rule was that no dirty politics were allowed. GE was still a team, and the success of the team was more important than the fates of the three men. He told them they were all highly capable of being great CEOs. He personally committed to them that if they could stand the heat and perform well, he would help each of them become CEO somewhere, though of course only one would succeed him at GE.

For six months, all three men played brilliantly, running their own businesses superbly and, at least overtly, supporting one another. When Welch picked Jeff Immelt on the Friday after Thanksgiving 2000, the other two reacted well in public, and shortly thereafter went to their new CEO posts: Nardelli became CEO of Home Depot and McNerney of 3M.

By all accounts, then, this successor fight was as open and clean as they come. Was it fair to the three men? Was it a good use of company resources—both human and material? Is there a better way of choosing the next company leader?

The answers to these questions may surprise you. First of all, this fight was *not* fair to the three men—they all had very different strengths and weaknesses and in the end there could only be one winner. But the fight *was* fair in the sense that it was played by rules and Welch made sure that the rules were fairly enforced. In the real world of business, there are winners and losers every day. It's not fair; it's just life.

Second, this was a very good use of company resources, because the need to find the best possible successor to Jack Welch was so vital to the company's future.

And third, while in some circumstances there are other good ways to pick the next leader of a company, none is automatically better than this one. The traditional exhaustive round of interviews and evaluations has a very low correlation with on-the-job success. Experience running other, similar businesses may or may not mean that an executive will find success in a new business. And should the experience be in a directly related field or something different? Many observers were puzzled when IBM chose Lou Gerstner, an RJR Nabisco executive with no experience in technology, to head that company. He went on to transform IBM and position it for enormous growth. No, it's not obvious that there is any single right way to pick a successor.

Welch's solution worked well, and in fact Immelt's first years on the job were successful during some very difficult and turbulent years.

In sum, Jack Welch did what good leaders need to do: he started a *right fight* about succession. Welch made two key moves: he consciously raised tensions and he created rules of the game to mitigate the consequences of those tensions. The process to pick a strong successor at GE was a very high-stakes one. It was worth a right fight—the future depended on it.

BOTH THE CAMPBELL Soup Company and GE stories point to some of the right things to fight over and some of the dangers that await those who deliberately create tensions in order to improve performance. At Campbell, there was much alignment work to do first. Then Conant had to keep vigilant, refereeing the fight to make sure that everyone focused on the right issues. Right fights can easily become wrong fights if the leadership doesn't guard against that outcome. Once you start a right fight, you have to see it through.

At GE, with so much at stake, the right fight for succession could very easily have turned into a wrong one. The three combatants might have turned on each other, or the rest of the organization might have become so mesmerized by the combat that it wasn't able to get anything done. Once Welch had launched the succession war, it was his job to see that the fighters played by the rules. He was the architect, conductor, and referee during the six months' fight.

Right fights must be fought over the right issues. And they must be waged according to a fair and reasonable set of rules of engagement. Our Right Fight Principles are comprehensive guidelines that enable you to choose the right fights and to fight them right. But before we delve into the principles, it's instructive to take a look at wrong fights—so we know what we want to avoid.

TWO

_____

Three Kinds of Fights
Not Worth Fighting

WRONG FIGHTS ARE the bane of organizational existence.
There are as many reasons for wrong fights as there are wrong
fights; as Tolstoy famously wrote, "Happy families are all alike;
every unhappy family is unhappy in its own way." The wrong
fights we highlight in this chapter are examples to give you a
sense of what to watch out for. If you don't see an organization
similar to yours here, please don't make the mistake of thinking that the lessons from the cases we'll discuss don't apply to
your circumstances. Wrong fights occur in all sizes and shapes,
and they happen in all categories of organizations. They are
destructive wherever they occur—in business, industry, government, nonprofit bodies, and volunteer groups, too.

Overall, there are three main categories of fights to avoid:

- **wrong fights fought wrong**—battles lacking
  focus on core issues; dysfunctional leadership

- **right fights fought wrong**—big, important battles executed poorly
- **wrong fights fought right**—skillful execution on the wrong battlefield

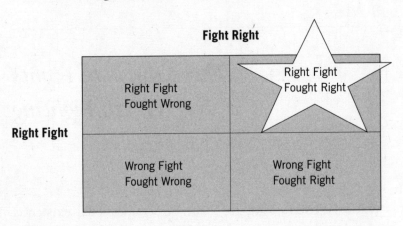

Good leaders intuitively fight right fights; great leaders create and manage them purposefully. In too many organizations, however, people fill the unhappy quadrants of the two-by-two matrix above. They focus on the right things but execute poorly. Or they expend superb execution skills on the wrong things. And from time to time we've all found ourselves in that worst of all possible fights—a badly managed, poorly chosen mess.

THE WRONG FIGHT FOUGHT WRONG

It's time to look at some case studies. In our first one, General Motors focused on the wrong things and executed poorly—a case of a wrong fight fought wrong. The *fight* was wrong because the market shifted and GM failed to shift with it. The fight was *fought wrong* because GM's rigid hierarchical structure didn't allow it to change in the ways it needed to fast enough.

CASE STUDY: *GM Fails to Shift Gears*

- Old thinking can blind people to the need for right fights about the future.
- Short-term successes often only postpone the need to deal with long-term issues.
- Rigid hierarchical organizational structure makes any change difficult.

It was the late 1980s. General Motors was struggling. But a line of sporty, rugged "sport utility vehicles" was one bright note in an otherwise dismal product spectrum. These cars were built on the small pickup truck chassis that GM had been selling for some time. The executives at GM decided to try a similar line of vehicles based on their large pickup truck chassis. In a way, it was a simple product extension move, but it created the full-size sport utility vehicle, a tremendous surge in business for GM (and the other Detroit carmakers), and sowed the seeds of its eventual downfall.

In 1990, GM directed that its Janesville, Wisconsin, plant stop making small cars and begin to make the new full-sized SUVs. The plant was retooled, and one Suburban after another began to roll off the assembly line. The huge, gas-guzzling seven-passenger behemoth was one of the most successful cars GM had ever launched. Initial production was 33,000 in the first year. Soon, the plant produced 200,000 per year. A second plant was retooled to make the SUVs. GM, Ford, Chrysler, and other firms around the world raced to offer bigger, more gadget-laden SUVs with three times as many cup holders as passenger seats.

GM, which lost money on many of its passenger cars, was making something like $10,000 to $15,000 per car on the SUVs. Small wonder that SUVs became the tail wagging the Detroit dog. By 2003, at the top of the market, GM was producing 680,000 Suburbans, Tahoes, Escalades, and Hummers per year. The SUV tapped into the "bigger is better" suburban demographic replete with McMansions and soccer moms ferrying their kids from the playing fields to the malls. But the company's short-term success was no match for its very long-term troubles.

The first sign of real trouble came in late summer 2005, when gas prices spiked in the aftermath of Hurricane Katrina. SUV sales tanked along with the rise in gas prices. The reversal came at a particularly bad time for GM. It was in the middle of reshaping its North American operations to address declining market share in everything except SUVs, and it was counting on the revenues from the gas-guzzlers to carry it through the expensive redesign.

Instead, gas prices briefly came down, and then headed into the stratosphere—just as GM was getting set to relaunch the SUV on a somewhat more fuel-efficient platform. In April of

2008, the GM board scrapped the plans. It closed the Janesville, Wisconsin, plant for good. GM had finally woken up to the new reality, and began belatedly to think about expanding its small-car capacity. Unfortunately, that thinking was too little, too late. The company failed, and filed for "controlled bankruptcy" in mid-2009. Given government funding, GM has a chance to reset and restart—but the GM of the past is gone for good. Indeed, its continued existence remains highly uncertain.

It would be easy to blame GM's troubles on the country's broader economic problems and the credit crisis that caused new car sales to plummet to their lowest point in decades. But it is important to remember that GM's woes were in reality the result of decades of right fights avoided—the inability to come up with an economically realistic settlement with the United Auto Workers, an aging manufacturing infrastructure that simply could not compete with the greenfield plants foreign competitors built in the United States, and most important a culture that encouraged executives to reward temporary success over winning longer term battles in cost, quality, fuel efficiency, and new technology. GM's rigid hierarchical bureaucracy prevented it from nimbly responding to the changing market.

"We made so much money on these vehicles for so long, I guess we just didn't see it coming," said one GM executive. That comment can be taken as the classic utterance of someone who was blinded by the initial success of his business model—and handcuffed by an unwillingness to change. Lawmakers, commentators, industry experts, and other automobile manufacturers had been discussing, thinking about, and planning on rising gas prices and smaller, more fuel-efficient cars for years. The evidence was plain for everyone else to see, but GM refused to see it.

Successful business models and winning marketing dogmas can have a potentially disastrous hold over executives, even entire companies. One of the most powerful and therefore dangerous truths about leadership is that leaders have to pick which battles to fight, which causes to champion. And they pick at the expense of other, often equally valid causes. Success can make it very hard for leaders and their organizations to see the contrary evidence when things start to go downhill.

THE RIGHT FIGHT FOUGHT WRONG

In the next case, Carly Fiorina of Hewlett-Packard (HP) focused on the right things, but couldn't execute effectively— an example of a right fight fought wrong.

CASE STUDY: *Carly Fiorina Makes Herself the Centerpiece of a Marketing Campaign*

- CEOs must remain referees of right fights, not fighters in them.
- In picking right fights, you must not ignore the history and traditional excellence of an organization.

Carly Fiorina fell into a classic CEO trap at HP. She was brought in because of her marketing expertise. Her early days with the company were widely lauded as revolutionary, game changing, and all about shaking up a company that was too engineering-centric. The result was that no one either outside or inside—at least at first—raised a skeptical eyebrow when a company with well-deserved and time-tested expertise in engineering tried to become a marketing machine.

Then came the Compaq acquisition.

There is considerable debate over the merits of Fiorina's protracted and high-stakes fight to buy Compaq Computer. For some, it looked strategically brilliant, and perhaps it might have been. But once the deal was done, the fact that mattered in the end was that she simply could not make it work.

How did Fiorina come to this sorry pass? She began her working life as a Kelly Girl, joined AT&T in 1980, and rose through the ranks to become a vice president. Her jump to corporate stardom came with the spin-off of Lucent Technologies, the research and development arm of AT&T, in 1996. She joined HP in 1999, shortly before the tech bubble burst and the pressure on companies like HP to find ways to continue to grow became intense.

Her tenure was marked by the early spin-off of Agilent Technologies and a massive layoff of 7,000 employees during the 2001 downturn. In 2002, she proposed the buyout of Compaq, a move that briefly put HP into the leadership position of sellers of personal computers.

But the merger was marked by the wholesale departure of Compaq's senior management, inconsistent earnings, and lackluster stock performance. The dominance and growth of the personal computer market that Fiorina hoped for from the merger never materialized. Moreover, HP's culture and Compaq's proved to be an uneasy match.

Innovation was not forthcoming. The combined company could not seem to get out of its own way and execute. Too much change, some said. Too little attention to what makes us great, others said. And at the top, Fiorina couldn't get the company redirected to deliver on what she had promised stakeholders in her hard-fought proxy battle.

In addition, having fought the Compaq battle in a way that left enemies lurking in many quarters, she did not set out to rebuild and repair the combined new organization. Instead, believing more stridently that she was right and the crucial center of a massive transformation, she pushed harder into the limelight, putting herself at the head of a huge sales and marketing effort, when what the company really needed to master was how to bring technology to market quickly and efficiently.

Fiorina believed in the power of her personal brand to get things working. But it didn't happen. The sales and marketing attempt to recharge a stagnating marketplace and a lackluster product mix failed to produce results.

Both companies' historic strengths were in engineering technology, not sales and marketing, and Fiorina failed to play to those strengths. There was nothing inherently wrong with pushing the company to match its engineering prowess by developing a powerhouse marketing capacity. But Fiorina made a fundamental mistake by making herself the iconic centerpiece of the marketing program, because it ultimately short-circuited her ability to provide clear and effective leadership.

Once she became HP's poster child, she could no longer design, orchestrate, or referee the necessary right fights within and among the sales, marketing, and engineering camps with any credibility, internally or externally. It was a setup for failure.

It's essential for a leader who starts creative ventures that should be right fights to remain the referee, in order to be able to manage the fights effectively. Failure to do so can easily doom the fights to becoming about faction, influence, and corporate politics rather than about the original subject of the fight itself.

Iconic leaders with big visions are found in all sectors, including education and nonprofit organizations. Often, their outsized personality and vision are called upon for fund raising, visibility of cause, and attracting talent. But you have to be careful. As a classic example of a right fight fought wrong in the nonprofit sector, we look at Larry Summers's troubled presidency of Harvard University in the early 2000s.

CASE STUDY: *Larry Summers Does It His Way at Harvard*

- Taking on a right fight is only the beginning; you also have to fight it right.
- An insistence on pushing his own personal agenda undermined his credibility and his ability to navigate the academic leadership terrain.

To understand why Larry Summers promised to be such a powerful agent for change at Harvard University, and why he failed to lead that change, you need to know a little about the history of the almost-375-year-old institution.

Harvard's fourteenth school, the Harvard School of Engineering and Applied Science, was officially welcomed into the fold only in 2007, promoted from being a mere division before that. Most other major universities had long since created schools of engineering and applied science, marking the general shift of the last century from the arts to the sciences in influence, money, prestige, and innovation.

But change comes slowly to this institution, and the university has struggled to live up to the reputation it established during the remarkable forty-year presidency of Charles William Eliot from 1869 to 1909. Eliot's name was universally recognized across America and indeed the world in a way that would startle us today. He presided over a number of academic reforms and innovations that still influence modern university life, such as elective courses and small classes for discussion. He lectured widely, wrote for magazines and other periodicals, and made himself and Harvard household words representative of intellectual ambition and achievement.

Harvard today retains an enormous reputation—it is the most widely recognized university in the world, and a world leader in many fields—but within its hallowed halls, many of its leaders struggle with stark realities of changes in education and research for which Harvard seems unprepared.

The unofficial motto of Harvard is "every tub on its own bottom," referring to the understanding that the schools will be separately run, funded, and organized. This fundamental approach, a cornerstone of Harvard's greatness for many years, has today become a barrier, preventing the school from functioning in the ways that leading universities need to operate in the twenty-first century.

The problem, of course, is that interdisciplinary knowledge and collaboration in sciences, arts, humanities, medicine, law, government, and business are fundamental drivers of today's greatest breakthroughs and inventions. This world is moving much faster than Harvard can.

Until recently, for example, it was literally true that every school within the university had its own calendar. Teaching an interdisciplinary course is difficult if you can't even agree on when the term starts and finishes!

Because of their vaunted independence, the schools have found it difficult to answer many questions that don't puzzle other universities for long: What does it mean to be part of a department? Or a field of study? Or a school? How can we best support our leading thinkers? What happens to funding? To peer review? To models for developing the next generation?

Into this maelstrom of complacency, introspection, and self-interest came Larry Summers in 2001. He was brought in as president in part to take Harvard from its time-honored traditions into leadership in the twenty-first century, including curricular redesign and cross-discipline collaboration.

Summers had many forward-looking ideas. For example, he wanted to get Harvard professors, some of whom are notorious for not taking much interest in undergraduates, to take their instructional duties more seriously, and to revamp the core curriculum to keep the Harvard curriculum the best in the world.

Furthermore, he wanted to start offering tenure to outstanding younger professors who appeared to have the potential for intellectual breakthroughs in the coming decades, rather than continuing Harvard's traditional practice of hiring those who have led the breakthroughs of the recent past. By waiting until academicians had proved themselves in the world of ideas, Harvard risked acquiring famous names only after they were past their prime.

Taking on these time-honored traditions for the purpose of furthering education and research were right fights. President Summers had excellent intentions.

But Summers attempted to achieve change the same way he had risen as a young faculty member—by being the smartest person in the room.

Indeed, he had ample claim to the title. Summers entered the Massachusetts Institute of Technology at age sixteen and was tenured at Harvard at twenty-eight—one of the youngest to be so honored in Harvard's history. He's the recipient of the John Bates Clark Medal for his work in macroeconomics; the prize is second only to the Nobel Prize in prestige among economists. He served as chief economist for the World Bank from 1991 to 1993, and secretary of the treasury under President Clinton from 1999 to 2001. Shortly after that, he assumed the presidency at Harvard.

But being the smartest person in the room doesn't necessarily make someone a good president. The role of Harvard's president must be to create an environment where other smart people want to be present, where there is openness to differing views and real collegial give and take when decisions need to happen. Unfortunately, Summers trusted only his own personal agenda. He seemed almost unable to understand what it takes to influence and motivate a body of very smart individuals.

He took on a popular professor of African American studies, accusing him of superficiality in his work, and saw him resign and go to rival Princeton. He took on half the world's population with inflammatory remarks on gender at a conference on women and science. And in meeting after meeting, he spent more time pushing his own ideas than listening to and encouraging the ideas of others.

In putting forward his own ideas so aggressively, Summers failed to energize others to join with him. In fact, he did quite the opposite: he pushed them to use their many tools and resources to resist him at every turn. The insistence that his was the only way forward doomed his efforts to failure from the start. He was asked to step down after only five years, with little to show in terms of tangible progress toward the visionary change he had wanted to create. Although in some contexts a very authoritarian style can be an asset, Summers simply couldn't see that that particular style was ill-suited to Harvard.

THE WRONG FIGHT FOUGHT RIGHT

For a classic illustration of a good organization gone wrong—and a wrong fight fought right—let's return to the corporate world and Dell.

CASE STUDY: *Dell Continues to Fight an Old Fight—and Loses*

- Too much alignment can kill you just as much as none at all.
- You have to allow dissent when times are good—it's just too hard when all hell is breaking loose.

Dell senior leaders shared a widespread—but mistaken—belief that the most important answer to an organization's performance challenges is fostering more alignment. Not meeting your numbers? Bring in a consultant and get everyone aligned on the mission and values. Translate that into performance targets and metrics. Even better, get everyone in life jackets and take them white-water rafting. That should take care of the problem, right?

In fact, that effort usually dampens constructive debate. Combined, these two tendencies—encouraging alignment and silencing meaningful debate—can lead to ruin.

When Dell burst on the scene in 1985 with the Turbo PC, selling for $800, the computer and the company were instant hits. Dell grossed $73 million in its first year, selling direct to consumers. The company went from strength to strength, and soon Dell computers were a fixture on the corporate and university scenes.

By 1992, *Fortune* magazine was including Dell in its list of the 500 largest companies in the world. By 1996, the company began selling computers directly via the Web. By 1999, it was the biggest seller of personal computers in the world.

The company forged its success out of its direct-sales model, just-in-time manufacturing, a highly efficient supply chain, and alignment. All was well until 2005, when, after a series of market expansions into products beyond personal computers, Dell stumbled.

When Kevin Rollins, then CEO of Dell, was confronted with lackluster growth and declining performance that year, his response was predictable but ineffective. Rollins had managed the company's explosive growth in the mid-1990s by pulling the levers of alignment hard. A brilliant consultant, he had polished the company's direct, build-to-order model to perfection.

Rollins sincerely believed that the way to win was through flawless execution—execution that required all employees to understand exactly how they fit into the larger scheme of things. At one point, the company created hundreds if not thousands of different variants of pocket cards that illustrated how each individual employee affected the company's return on invested capital. It's difficult to find a more extreme example of strategic alignment driven down to frontline workers.

But increasingly, Dell's problem was lackluster growth, not poor return on capital.

Rollins's attempts to replicate the company's successful direct PC model didn't work nearly as well in consumer product markets like flat-screen TVs. It's not that the company's strategic alignment was wrong. Dell could manufacture and distribute the new products very cost effectively. But the new product strategy revealed a simple truth about the company that its analysts and own executives sometimes found easy to forget. Dell was a highly successful direct-sales company, but not a particularly successful direct-to-consumer company.

The lion's share of Dell sales and market share was attributed to relatively sophisticated corporate buyers who knew exactly what they wanted to buy and didn't value after-sales support over the 10 percent savings they achieved by buying direct. The same assumptions don't hold true in the very different world of consumer electronics, especially for big ticket items like flat-screen TVs, where people want to see the product in a store before they actually buy one, and where quality and timeliness of services after the product is purchased matter a lot.

Dell had expanded beyond a marketplace that it understood well and was trying to woo customers with an approach that didn't work. Although there were leaders who questioned the company's strategy, their voices carried little weight when stock prices were high and the entire management team was held together by stock option plans that promised life-changing levels of personal wealth.

Connecting senior management tightly to company success with these kinds of incentives is management dogma in thousands more companies than Dell. It is the stuff of business school courses, consultants' recommendations, and favorable mention in the press. In fact, to suggest anything else risks accusations of heresy. Why shouldn't executives' returns be tied to the company's? Doesn't that align their interests, and isn't that the best way to ensure good, reliable performance quarter after quarter? The answer is yes—but only until a given strategy has run its course.

In fact, Dell was attempting to grow into new markets with new rules, and that required substantial changes to its strategy and its business model. It was unable to switch from the model that had produced its spectacular successes in PCs.

By all accounts Dell was not an easy company to work for. Executives put in long hours and managed myriad corporate processes to ensure that everyone remained aligned with the overall goals of the organization.

It was a victim of too much alignment.

Sales growth had leveled off in its core markets, and Dell was struggling to find new ones in an effort to meet Wall Street's demand for ever-increasing sales. In a very real sense, Dell was crippled by its success.

The Dell story illustrates the roller-coaster ride that wrong fights can create. Rollins's troubles began during tremendous prosperity for the company, but ended in less than two years in a period of extraordinary public criticism, poor stock price performance, and the inevitable wholesale departure of his senior team. Money or the promise of it has tremendous power to attract and retain talent. Unfortunately, the converse is also true. People who came to the company on the promise of becoming rich were extremely unlikely to stay once that promise seemed doubtful.

Rollins himself left the company convinced that the stock was undervalued and that his strategy would be proven right. Once in a crisis, the external pressure that leaders like Rollins face makes it difficult, if not impossible, to encourage the right level of strategic debate.

The seeds of that debate existed for years within the Dell

management team. There were dissenting voices and senior level departures—including the head of marketing—before the company fell on hard times. But no one listened.

TRAPS THAT CREATE WRONG FIGHTS

In the cases we've just looked at there's a common thread. These are smart people. These are long-established or rapidly growing institutions. They seem to have the ingredients in place to succeed. Yet in spite of everything they had going for them, they found themselves in wrong fights that drained their organizational energy, distracted their leadership from both long-term goals and day-to-day operations, and disappointed stakeholders.

Why do smart people and good companies get into wrong fights? It's obvious that no clear-thinking person would intentionally set out to end up in a quagmire. But there are insidious traps in organizational life, traps that distract leaders from their conscious choices and plans and land them in wrong fights. Leaders are particularly likely to get trapped in three areas: misusing personal relationships, mismanaging structural alignment, and misjudging the business cycle.

Traps Involving Personal Relationships

One all-too-common example of the first kind of trap is *broken personal relationships*. The vice president of marketing is hired because he forms a close relationship with the CEO during rosy times of business expansion. Then he has a falling out with her when business slows and the CEO requires him to make some tough layoffs. Amidst the detritus of the personal politics, a wrong fight can easily develop over the layoffs. The issue can quickly morph from one about the right workforce for a slower market to one about turf wars, head counts, and personal fiefdoms.

Another common personal relationship trap arises when a person or team doesn't trust another person or team to complete critical work the group depends on for its activities. People typically resolve such problems with work-arounds. More than a few work-arounds and you have a profoundly dysfunctional organization. Work-arounds always mask wrong fights, and energy gets wasted in the process.

And what of the case we've all seen, when an obvious idiot gets promoted to a position of authority at least one level above his competence? Is he related to the chairman? A golfing buddy of the vice president of marketing? A chance meeting of the impulsive, spur-of-the-moment, do-it-now CEO? It could be any of these but the result is always the same—widespread resentment and more work-arounds. This personal relationship trap directs the energy of the organization toward compensating for failure. The effort wastes time, money, and organizational esprit.

Traps Involving Structural Misalignment

Not all traps involve personal relationships. Some traps are structural. Failure to align things that can be aligned is certainly a trap that can seduce leaders into wrong fights. If IT and the business divisions are sparring over what sort of information should be gathered to track business progress, then there is some alignment work to be done. If sales and R&D disagree about what new products are closest to market readiness, that's something that a good discussion can resolve. If several divisions bicker over budgetary allocations, choose a strategic direction and assign a division to lead the way.

Another structural trap occurs when translation issues trip up otherwise strategically aligned organizations when they try to apply their strategy to specific actions. That's when people realize they have big disagreements about how to implement a strategy that seemed clear enough when it was just talk.

Sales organizations often fall prey to the translation trap. Every year, sales organizations set quotas and establish rules in order to meet the targets set in annual strategy and review sessions. But translating targets into actionable guidelines for selling is complex work. Overweight sales to existing customers, and you'll get few new sales. Overreward new business, and your sales people will neglect your existing customers. Even when everybody agrees on the targets, translation errors focus attention on areas where interpretations differ, and wrong fights can be the result.

A final kind of structural trap occurs when the private agendas of influential leaders are allowed to distort organizations in ways that they are ill-equipped to handle. The CEO who relocates company headquarters to be near his ski chalet. The CIO who insists on a particular system because he's comfortable with it even though it's a poor fit for his organization. The board member who insists on a policy that makes no sense for current realities because it helped him when he was starting out in business. In each of these examples, there is an imbalance between the influence of the person in question and his or her formal authority that will cause a destructive wrong fight.

Traps Involving the Business Cycle

The last category of trap is probably the most difficult to guard against. The natural ups and downs of business create a *success → complacency → decline → failure → turnaround* cycle that is notoriously difficult to avoid and also extremely likely to lead the unwary into wrong fights.

One of the biggest of these business cycle traps is unrealistic outside expectations. This trap is particularly dangerous for the top brass, but it can affect every level of an organization. Let's say you're a CEO who has recently taken the reins of a slow-growth, mature company and the pressure is on to kickstart new growth. Through a combination of luck and serendipity, you achieve runaway sales of a couple of new products and a 30 percent growth trajectory. The problem is that your shareholders, the market, analysts, and the rest of the financial world now expect 30 percent growth year after year. The minute you fall to a relatively tragic 25 percent growth, you're in trouble.

The result? You're trapped, and you're tempted to swing for the fences every time with bold, innovative new products that will revolutionize the market. But what company can please a finicky marketplace again and again? It may be counterintuitive, but it's a wrong fight to strive for a blockbuster with every new product. No organization can take the pressure, and the expectation becomes destructive. The real goal of successful innovative organizations should be a succession of base hits.

Unfortunately, even a string of base hits can create a business cycle trap because success too often creates complacency that can erode productive tension. Runaway successes distort the systems and processes of an organization just as surely as failure does. Organizations with too much money face troubles equal to organizations with too little money.

Fundamentally, the problem with runaway success is that it creates institutional reluctance to question assumptions, contemplate change, or consider alternate futures. When CSC Index, the consulting company that rode to huge growth in earnings and employees on the back of reengineering, came to the end of the reengineering craze, it was woefully unprepared to deal with the change in circumstances. It went from 40 percent growth one year to red ink the next, and quickly sunk beneath the waves after that. It was simply unable to contemplate continuing under any scenario except rapid growth. It fought a series of wrong fights about personnel, platforms, and other inwardly focused issues, unable to refocus on its customers with new and innovative offerings.

It's the *Titanic* problem—the inability to imagine that things might be different, and thus the inability to act when they are, suddenly and catastrophically.

Similarly, alignment works so well in crisis situations that it can be hard to stop after the crisis is past. It's one of the reasons good turnaround leaders are often not successful in normal times. When the boat is sinking, everyone has to focus on bailing and getting the lifeboats ready. There's no room for experimentation about the future under these circumstances. Turnaround leaders are usually very good at getting people to commit, often at great personal sacrifices of time, money, and position, to saving the organization.

But once that's accomplished, the urge to continue in crisis mode can be hard to resist. Why start to allow for debate and discussion, experimentation and pilot projects, when the other way worked so well—and indeed saved the company?

Ultimately, of course, keeping a company in perpetual crisis will sap morale, lead to an exclusively short-term focus, and position the company poorly for the future. But on any given day, how do you decide that the crisis is over and it's time for normalcy to return?

AVOIDING THE TRAPS

It should be clear by now that avoiding wrong fights and picking right ones isn't as easy as looking at whether a company is currently doing well or poorly. The leadership trick is to avoid the extremes and instead to adopt a "never empty, never full" attitude. Knowing *where* and *when* to use tension is critical. Knowing *how* to work through the tension is equally important. Leaders have to see that right fights are fought right.

We begin learning about tensions and fights from infancy. Some of what we know is instinctive and even encoded in our biology. But the evolving human brain has a highly developed capacity to override our most primitive instincts. You are not stuck at the level of pure instinct or with the habits you developed unconsciously from life experience. Right fighting is learnable; it is a set of skills that you and your teams can acquire.

The Right Fight Principles in this book are designed to guide you in this quest. They will guide you in choosing what to fight about, and how to do it right. They apply across organizations large and small, in public and private sectors, in businesses, arts organizations, and government. They will help you to see where you currently are stuck, and applied collectively, they will enable you and your teams to consistently move to right fights fought right.

THREE

"Jack Sparr" Takes on a Right Fight

The story in this chapter is a composite story of real characters fighting real right fights that we have witnessed and been part of. While we've changed names and circumstances to preserve confidentiality, the essentials are true and take into account the human side of what it requires to engage in right fights—to struggle, to lead, to have setbacks, and to win.

JACK SPARR CALLED to order what was probably the most important meeting of his life. "Let's get started," he said. "You need to know what's going on."

He paused a moment and looked around at his team. He was proud of them. They were going to rise to the challenge. They had to. What was it that President Kennedy said about being an involuntary hero? *I had to; they sunk my boat.* They were all going to have to be heroes now.

"Here's the deal," Jack began. "Franz needs something extraordinary out of us this coming year. The company's under pressure to grow. A lot. And since we're the best unit in the company, we need to grow the most. Profitably. Thirty percent."

He held up his hand to stop the exclamations from his team. He was ready for it, of course; they had all worked so hard for so long.

Andre, Jack's head of marketing, cut through the noise with his dry voice. "It's not like we haven't been growing, Jack." There were murmurs of agreement around the big conference table.

"I know, I know," said Jack. "This is our reward for doing so well. But we've got a tremendous opportunity with the portable unit. Not only to sell a lot of product and make our numbers. But to save lives. And that's why we get up in the morning."

He looked around the table again, and saw that he had everyone's attention. "And that's why I know you're going to be able to do this. Despite the bad news."

He paused again.

"Don't tell me," said Andre. "No budget increase to make the 30 percent, right? No budget to launch a new product into new markets. Am I getting warm?"

"That's about right. We're getting some, but not as much as I wanted—or you wanted." Jack put his hands on the table. "I'm still negotiating with Franz and the other divisions, but it's looking like you can count on 5 percent at most."

Jack waited until the chorus of groans and exclamations had died down again, and then he continued. "That means that we have to figure out how to make the new product launch work, expand sales of the standard line, and do both at the same time with essentially the same amount of money as last year."

Jack paused. "Here's what I'm looking for. Andre, we just aren't going to have the budget to do the big worldwide splash for the portable model that you were looking for. So from you, I need a plan B to get us to thirty percent profitable growth in spite of that little limitation. And Danita." He turned to his SVP of sales. "I want the same thing from you and sales. Give us a plan to get to 30 percent assuming flat funding. You're not going to have the money for a big reorg, but let's see some creativity—let's see how much you can do." He paused again. "You've both got two weeks. And don't give me anything half-hearted or provincial. Your plans need to look at all aspects of what the division can bring to the table to deliver these results. Work with each other, too. You know the drill. You don't get a Coke by putting four quarters in four machines. Think big."

Everyone around the table rolled their eyes at this one; they'd heard it many times from Jack, who had found much of his success in his career by making big, gutsy bets. But they looked ready to try, thought Jack, his pride in his team surging.

"I know this is tough," he said, "But you guys are the best there is. I know you can do it. Two weeks from today. Same time, same place. Give it your best shot."

There was a brief silence. Then Danita spoke up. "We'd better get started, then," she said, with a light tone that fooled no one.

As he watched them go, Jack wondered how the competition he had just set in motion would go between Danita and Andre. They both were in line for his job, and the race between the two of them was fierce. He knew they would both take this opportunity as a way to show their stuff. That was in part why he had set them against each other. He just had to watch to make sure that it didn't get out of bounds. They were both tough, no-nonsense executives with a good team sense, but also a keen eye for self-interest. Jack was certain that the resulting plans would be better than either of them would produce without the competition, and he was as interested as they were in the results.

THE NEXT MORNING, stuck in traffic and late for a meeting that Andre had asked for "urgently," Jack found himself thinking again about what he was tasking his team to do.

He had forged a great team. His two SVPs of sales and of marketing especially had what it took—and they both knew it. But they kept their egos under control for the most part and worked well enough together, especially when he was in the room. Right now, he knew, they were aligned on the task and everyone was working as hard as they could.

So how were they going to get 30 percent growth and a decent profit to boot?

It all came down to the new portable model. They needed it to hit home runs around the world. How were they going to manage that?

If he pulled this off, he was in the running to get the top

job and to realize all the dreams he and Marcia had shared when they were first dating years ago. It would go a long way to healing the memories of the years of frequent moves and Marcia's difficulties in adjusting to first one community and then another. They could redo the summer house and he could . . .

Daydreaming. He had to concentrate on the meeting ahead. And the traffic, which wasn't moving.

He had thrown down the gauntlet to the team, and he had a lot of confidence in them and in their ability to get to a great solution. And the new portable unit had the potential to make a difference all over the globe. Merge us, or sell us, and it's not just us who lose, Jack thought. It's millions of people out there.

He knew the next few weeks were going to be tough on everyone, but it was worth it. They were fighting for a reason. And he was determined that it would be a fair fight, and that there would be something in it for everyone no matter the outcome.

Where was the big bet? That's what he wanted from Danita and Andre.

With more time and a bigger budget, it would of course be easy enough. But with such a tight time frame, and limited budget, how to get there? What were the key investments to make to get the jump in revenues? What was the right focus: existing products, the portable model that looked so promising, rationalizing the sales organization, or reorganizing marketing?

Jack knew that Danita and her sales organization would

develop a plan that incorporated both sales and marketing, but where the jump in performance came fundamentally from sales. Andre would likely do the same thing, but with the emphasis on a major marketing program, and he'd likely tie it tightly to certain sales leaders as well.

Jack was looking for a winner—a clean choice, based on the merits. He needed their best thinking and he needed to see what they would do. He needed that 30 percent, and they needed to get going.

He grimaced. The traffic had finally allowed him to pull near an exit and he suddenly gunned the Mustang's engine and took the ramp at speed. He was going to have to take the back roads or miss the meeting. He increased his speed, looking reflexively around for radar.

The '65 Mustang was his one indulgence, purchased after much deliberation when he was made head of the division. Marcia laughed at him and called it his midlife crisis cliché car, but how could he explain to her what was wrapped up in that automobile?

He knew it wasn't grown-up or dignified to still get a kick out of a car, but he didn't care. It was too much fun.

Jack finally pulled into the parking lot, sweating slightly, with a couple of minutes to spare. He would be on time after all.

He was already tense as he strode down the corridor to his office, offered a passing "Morning" to his assistant, Denise, and checked e-mail quickly before heading to the meeting with Andre.

"I don't know how long we'll be," he called to Denise as he walked by in the opposite direction. "If Franz calls, tell him I'll get back to him at lunch, okay?" The company CEO was pushing him hard to come up with something, and he was checking on progress frequently.

"Okay," Denise called to his back. "There's just one thing."

"What? I don't have time for a crisis." Jack wheeled back on her. He smiled, to lessen the effect of his abrupt words.

"You may want to make five minutes for this one. It's an irate customer tape you will want to hear."

"Irate customer? I really don't have time . . ."

"This is an irate $5 million customer," Denise cut in.

"Christ. Broder. Put it through to my office, hold the calls, and call down to Andre and tell him I'll be there in ten minutes, okay?"

"Okay." Denise was already punching buttons on the various machines on her desk.

Jack dashed back into his office, gave the door a kick shut, and settled into a chair at his conference table with a groan. He picked up the receiver, pressed a few buttons, and put the recorded call on speakerphone.

A really angry voice washed over him. Jack concentrated hard on it, on what it was saying. Basically, Jack began to hear, one of Danita's reps had completely screwed up, if the angry voice of his second-biggest customer was to be believed. Deliveries were late, installations were slapdash, and the training they had promised wasn't happening.

How could Danita have let it get this bad? She never let something like this slip past her. "Attention to detail" would be written on her tombstone.

What made him really angry was that he didn't have time to deal with the issue properly right then, and he hated to let something like this go, even for a few hours.

He was at the end of the tape, and he was not a happy camper.

"Denise!" He knew he was bellowing, but he didn't care.

"Yes—sir?" Denise was at the door, instantly.

That calmed down Jack a little.

"Call Broder. Be really, really, nice to him. Say I want to speak to him personally this afternoon if possible. Tell him we'll make him whole. Not to worry. We're on it. I'm handling it personally. Something like that. Okay?"

"Got it. No problem." Denise could be all business when she wanted to be. Jack appreciated that.

"Thanks. You're one in a million. I've gotta go."

"You're welcome." Denise was already heading back to her desk and Jack took the first deep breath he'd taken in a while.

He stood up, trying to clear his mind of everything that was getting in the way of the meeting with Andre, and headed off down the hall.

ABOUT TEN MINUTES later, Jack was scowling. Andre was having a rare crisis of confidence, pointing out that Danita knew everyone and was likely to get more support for her plan—including resources to work on it. Somehow, Danita was going to use her popularity to game the system and make it impossible for his approach to get a fair hearing.

"Andre," Jack said, finally cutting him off, "This isn't the way the game is played. If Danita does try to pull a fast one, don't you think I'd notice? Everyone knows that I'm watching to make sure the whole team gives their best resources to both of you, fairly. And your groups need to work together as well. I've clearly asked both of you to think about the whole division, and not just your area."

Jack shifted impatiently in his chair. "If you need help, let me know. I agree, Danita is a hell of a presenter, but that doesn't make her anything but talented. Life isn't fair. But your work will get a fair shake. It's your job to see that your true brilliance, something we have relied on for a long time, is out there in full form. And please don't present one of your infamous PowerPoint decks and put us all to sleep."

He got up to show that it was time to go. For Andre, it had to be enough.

"You've got two weeks," said Jack as he left Andre's office. "Make the most of it."

JACK WAS GLAD the waiting was over. He had spent the time—at least it seemed that way to him—putting out little political fires started by Andre and Danita. Andre had gone a little ornery under the pressure and started rumors about sales and how it was not actually meeting targets now, so how could it meet any new, higher ones? Danita was using all the force of her personality to get the best resources she could.

The tricks had shown Andre and Danita in a new light to Jack, but he was focused at the moment on making the best decision possible on the merits. He would give them both feedback and coaching later. The stakes were so high he didn't want anyone feeling railroaded. But time was running out. He had let Danita and Andre go long enough; it was time to have the presentations, get the two ideas out on the table, and make an executive decision.

"Danita," said Jack, smiling, "You're first. Go ahead. Knock it out of the park."

As Jack listened first to Danita's and then Andre's presentations, the starkness of the choice became clear in his mind. The two teams had gone in very different directions.

Andre had hired a top-notch consultant with wide expertise in marketing. The consultant had come back with a market segmentation plan that could hit the numbers. And the plan was a good one. Their basic insight was to goose up the base business a little, but to take most of the money and do a big rollout of the new portable model, taking on the middle market of small businesses, local organizations, schools, and even a piece of the consumer market in a big way for the first time.

Jack recognized that the plan would work in theory, but he was nervous about pushing the sales force into the middle market and consumer arenas, where they didn't have much experience. They had always been focused on the larger B2B world.

Danita's plan was heading in an entirely different direction. She was arguing that the main effort should be on the sales force, to reorganize them regionally. Danita had some research that showed that the base business could be focused that way and take a huge leap. The good news was that the base business had much better margins than the portable units.

Her idea was to use the profits in the first year to build up the portable model's major expansion in Year Two, because she was convinced that was going to take more time. She was going to need big resources quickly to pull off the restructuring, add a few high-priced top people, and to put up a Web front end for the sales force, to help them with the portable unit rollout in Year Two. It wouldn't completely gut the marketing budget, but she was going to need a big piece of it.

The choice lay with him. And the team knew it. The tension had been building slowly, and Jack could feel it. Something in his gut told him that it wasn't a bad thing, even though he knew there was a certain amount of tea-leaf reading going on.

It was obvious that both Danita and Andre had agendas, but that was okay—it was just reality. Everyone understood that. They also wanted the whole team to succeed—so while there would be a winner and a loser, it wouldn't be the end of the world for the loser. And Jack would make sure that the loser would get something, too.

He smiled to himself. His HR guy had suggested a team-building exercise—one of those dumb rafting trips—to help with the tension. But Jack thought the stakes were higher than just playing nice. This was worth doing because they were aiming for something really significant. A little tension along the way was worth the game.

"Thanks, Danita," Jack concluded. "Thanks, Andre. That

was fabulous. You've given us all a lot to think about over lunch and after, and I'm sure we'll have lots to talk about this afternoon. Shall we all reconvene at one?" He looked around the room, seeing nods and agreement, nodded back, picked up his BlackBerry and his pile of papers, and left to head back to the office. He needed time to figure out what he thought about the two ideas. More important, what was the big bet that would make the numbers, profitably, and involve both sales and marketing?

Jack knew that there would be some hurt feelings whichever path he chose. But more important, there was the feeling in his gut. As good as Danita's presentation was, it didn't feel completely solid. It didn't seem strong enough to bet the farm on, and that's what was going to happen. Her plan didn't make enough of the new machine. He knew it was going to be big, and her plan went with it too slowly. If they waited, essentially, until Year Two, a competitor might get the jump on them.

And Andre's plan was just the opposite—too much pressure on the portable machine. But everything in Jack's experience told him that a big bet was essential. They couldn't bet half the farm on each plan. That wouldn't get them anywhere.

Jack sighed. He had to think about this. He would have to take the time. No matter if the team screamed for a decision. They would have to wait a little longer. Sometimes the top guy had to ask that of the team. The stakes were high, and he had to get the decision right.

•　•　•

THE NEXT WEEK, Jack, on a plane to the World Economic Forum, found himself thinking over the presentations Danita and Andre had made. They both were good—Danita's was great, actually—and his organization was looking to him for a decision. It wasn't anything they said, exactly; it was the way they all looked at him. He knew that they were thinking, why don't you just decide? He was famous for making big bets. Why wasn't he ready to jump one way or the other?

That thought took him all the way to Davos.

"JACK! HOW THE hell are you?" A loud, cheery voice broke into his thoughts as Jack waited for the first session to begin. He looked up.

"Geoff! I didn't know you'd be here! I'm great, and how about you? Still not indicted?" It was his old friend from business school. They had met in an ethics class and had a running joke about which of them was going to be the first to run afoul of a law neither of them had ever heard of.

"I'm running the division, now," said Geoff, with pardonable pride.

"That's great. So am I," Jack replied.

They soon fell into reminiscences about their times together at INSEAD, and Jack felt himself relaxing for the first time in weeks as he traded stories with his old friend.

"So what's eating you?" Geoff finally asked, looking at him directly.

"Nothing. What do you mean?"

"You only look like you've been hung in a smokehouse for a week. Don't try to bull me. What's going on?"

Jack took a deep breath and told Geoff the story of his ultimatum and his need to make the right bet.

Geoff listened intently, and then said something that surprised Jack. "Maybe this time you can't make one of your big bets. I know, I know, that's always worked for you before. But maybe your gut is telling you something important. Maybe it's time for you to think differently."

"What do you mean?" asked Jack. "I can't just combine the two. Then I'd have a half-assed sales program and a half-assed marketing push, given the budget."

"No, listen to me," said Geoff, his voice rising. "Sometimes to win big, you have to do something different than what you've done in the past. Get off your high horse. Think about it differently. I don't know what the answer is, but you do— somewhere in that expanding gut of yours." He said this last with a smile, and the two of them started reminiscing about their b-school days again.

BACK FROM DAVOS, Jack was heading to Franz's office to reassure him that his team was fine, in spite of the rumbles the CEO was hearing around the building.

And he was planning to announce that he was going with Danita's plan.

But when he got to the corner office, something in him told him to hold back.

"There's a lot riding on this," Jack said to Franz. "I've got one shot, and I want to get it right. That's why I've started this little competition between the two of them. They're good executives. They can handle it. And I'm going to wrap it up soon, so the agony will be over."

"What about the fallout?" wondered Franz. "What are you going to do about the loser?"

"We can make them whole," Jack said. "This is going to work, Franz. I know it. There will be plenty of glory to go around for everyone."

Franz looked at him. "You sound confident."

"I am," said Jack. "This is going to work. I need 'til the end of the week."

"I'm looking forward to it," said Franz. "There's just one other thing. What the hell is going on with Broder? I don't need to tell you he's our biggest customer for the old model. We can't afford to alienate him."

"I've got it covered," Jack reassured him. "Danita's folks were spread a little thin. But we've double-teamed Broder and we've got him back on track."

"I'm glad to hear it," said Franz, as the two men stood and Jack took his leave.

THAT NIGHT, TRYING to fall asleep next to Marcia, Jack was still debating with himself. *What's wrong with me?* he wondered. *Is Geoff right? Do I need to think in some new way? But big bets have always worked for me. There's gotta be some way to make a big bet that pays off this time, too.*

Suddenly Jack sat up in bed. He pounded the pillow. "That's it!"

Marcia stirred beside him. "Mmmmmm?" She said, sleepily. "What's up?"

"Sorry, hon," said Jack, as soothingly as he could. "Just thinking. Sorry. Go back to sleep."

THE NEXT MORNING, sitting in his office with the October light streaming in through the window making the dust motes dance over his conference table, Jack found himself reaching for the phone.

"Get me Sascha, please," he said into the phone. A minute later, he heard the voice of his old friend and mentor. "Sascha," he said, "let me run an idea past you. Tell me if I'm crazy. Let me put you on speaker phone."

An hour later, Sascha was still encouraging him to trust his gut. "Geoff is right," she said. "It's time to look at this differently. You're in a truly complex situation here, but I think you've got an opportunity to get what's best out of both plans—the markets, margins, and timing sensitivities require it. But it means that you'll have constant trade-offs throughout the year—things you will have to stay on top of. Give it back to the team. Give them the challenge. They're good, in spite of the politics. They'll come through for you. Trust them. Trust your gut."

When Jack hung up, he was already thinking harder than he had ever thought before.

• • •

AN HOUR LATER, the veins on his neck were bulging as Jack shouted at Danita, "How could this not be resolved? This is worth $5 million to us! Franz is all over me!"

Danita kept her cool. "We're on it. Maybe I was trying to handle it too low-level. I was trusting Alex with the fix. It's time for him to learn how to play the big game. I guess he wasn't moving fast enough."

"He must have been moving pretty damn slow for Broder to call me again! He's not exactly the communicative type! I just don't want to learn that he's going with Consolidated Instruments!"

"Jack, I give you my word," said Danita soothingly. She continued, "This will be resolved by end of day. Broder will be smiling again. And he won't be calling. Let me go and hold Alex's hand."

"Go," said Jack, already feeling a little better. He trusted Danita to fix it when she gave her word.

"Hey," he yelled out to Denise as soon as Danita had gone. "I'm going to catch a five-minute meeting with Andre. I ran into him and he asked for a quick one. Hold my calls."

"What about your wife?" Denise said as he strode past her.

Jack screeched to a halt. "Why, what's up?"

"Jimmy's been kicked out of school."

"What!" Jack felt something lurch inside him.

"Just kidding," said Denise. "He's not feeling well. He's coming home early. Marcia's got him. Everything's okay, but she wants to check in with you."

"One of these days, you're going to give me a heart attack,"

Jack muttered as he resumed his stride, reaching for his cell phone.

Five minutes later, he was once again on his way to see Andre.

Jimmy was actually not feeling well, and had been put to bed after chicken soup and a cuddle. Marcia was on the case.

On his way to Andre's office, he wondered what Andre would try to do. Jack knew from his back channels that the betting was on Danita, and Andre was worried. He had to keep an eye on both of them at this point to make sure that no one stepped out of line. And it was time to astonish them both and get them to work out a whole new approach—not a compromise, but something that took into account the complexity of regions, markets, and segments. They needed to come together on the best of both, without the dreaded half of each. That he would not tolerate. Something like the ideas he had sketched out the night before and while talking to Sascha. For the first time in his career, he was thinking about big bets differently, like two intertwined strands instead of one big choice. He was willing to risk it—he felt tired, and yet deeply excited at the same time.

"Andre, you wanted to see me?" Jack said, smiling, as he walked into Andre's office.

FIVE MINUTES LATER, Jack was no longer smiling. Andre had delivered an earful. And Jack didn't like what he heard. Andre had begun with a long, involved story about his design group. They had come up with beautiful packaging for the portable model, but the supply chain folks were pointing out that it was too expensive. They were suggesting an alternative plastic housing that wouldn't support the colors in the gorgeous design. Andre had wound up the story by looking at him expectantly. But Jack wasn't going to intervene on his behalf. This was a wrong fight, and Jack knew it right away. Andre was a brilliant creative, but he was so ornery—and here he was, making another land-grab for power. No, he could be brilliant but wrong, and Jack was going to have to make that clear to him, again.

Andre then jumped into an attack on Danita's proposal that involved mainly questioning her team's ability to handle the retraining that would be necessary. It was dirty pool, and Jack could see it from a mile away, but he heard Andre out because he needed the marketing genius to be a team player when Jack put forward his new approach that afternoon. Everyone was going to have to grow—especially Andre, thought Jack.

So Jack merely said that it would be time to worry about the training when the plan was set, and got up to signal the meeting was over. As he left, he thought to himself that it was time to change the tensions. Walking back to his office, he caught sight of himself in the glass windows. Looking into his own eyes, he wondered if there was something about himself that was making this too hard. Was there a way that would be easier on everyone? *Self-doubt*, he said to himself, *is just part of the territory of leadership. I've been here before. But no, that's not right. I've done my homework—I really understand the issues. I have a great team. I'm up for this challenge—it's worthy of the work, the stress, the ways we will all have to grow.*

"WHAT WILL REALLY move the top line and get us to 30 percent growth?" Jack looked at his team, including Danita and Andre in his gaze. "I know I always say that you don't get a Coke by putting four quarters in four machines."

There were some just-audible groans around the table. Jack ignored them. He had expected as much.

"But," Jack continued, "I've really been struggling with that idea this time. Both of your plans make big bets. You did what I asked. But my gut has been telling me that neither one is going to work the way we want it to." Jack paused. "So I'm going to surprise you this time. I've come to realize that this fight has brought out two great options, but it has also made me see that it's more complex than we originally thought. Your approaches both have brilliant aspects and we need both—not half of each. There is a way to get to 30 percent, but it's going to involve the two of you working together, with your teams, to come up with a new plan that does both—reorganize the geography, and bet on the portable model. With a sensitivity to timing, local realities, and a new look at segmentation, I know it will work. We need to interweave this plan and not expect one global approach all at the same time. It's got to work—it's got the potential to save a lot of lives, and our company is counting on us. So I'm going to ask you both, once again, to come up with a plan—but this time a joint one."

He looked at Danita and Andre and their teams. Everyone

had been poised for a winner and a loser. But now they had something new to think about. Both teams were silent, looking at each other. And then, to Jack's surprise, Andre spoke first.

"Danita," he said, "I've been putting marketing first because I really believed it was the way to go, and I haven't been entirely open with you. But Jack's just asked us to do something that's really important. I don't fully understand it yet, but if Jack is willing to think beyond what's worked for him before, I am, too. And in an intuitive way, I can feel this will work. Of course, it will save lives, and it could be really big for us. That's why I got into this business, and I know you care about it, too. What do you say? Can we work together on this?"

Danita looked at him in silence for a long minute. Finally she said, "Welcome back, Andre. I was hoping the genius marketer I know and love would get back in town. Let's get to work."

Jack realized he had been holding his breath. He let it out. "Danita, your plan makes sense, because we need to roll out the new machine in stages. And you're right that the standard models get us the margins we need at first to keep this ball rolling. And that we can do much more with existing models, especially in certain regions. We'd be leaving money on the table not to do this. But Andre's right, too—we've got to bet on the new machine, and bet big, or there will be no tomorrow. So here's what I've been able to figure out so far. We need to roll out the geographies in phases. We need to tailor the marketing program for each new area and get much more sophisticated about segmentation, fast. And Danita and Andre, together, you've got to figure out how to bring the sales team up to speed quickly enough to make this happen. Marketing will be all over this in support of what you need. We're going to do both plans, we're just going to do them intertwined, in stages. What this means is that we won't have one easy answer, like a formula, for how we decide priorities. We'll have to work this every step of the way—encouraging different views and sorting out competing priorities as things emerge and we learn more. This will take the combined focus and attention of the three of us, and I'm committed to giving this as much of my time and attention as it needs. This is still a big bet, but it's the best of both worlds."

Jack sat back and waited, as both teams considered the implications of what he had just said. Finally, Danita spoke. "I'm ready to get to work. Andre, you'll have my input on which geographies to take first by tomorrow. We can set up a rolling training program that will take us around the world. What do you say?"

She looked at Andre. After a moment, Andre slowly nodded his head. "Let's get started," he said.

"Great," said Jack. "Let's see the new plan on my desk in three days."

The two teams, refocused and reenergized, got going on the new direction, and with Jack, Danita, and Andre working closely, they solved the problems, one by one. They actually enjoyed working together, so they were able to heal the tensions of the previous weeks quickly.

The energy was so great that people in ops, logistics, and distribution quickly got on board as well.

The double-stranded plan and ensuing rollouts were an extraordinary success, and the team went on to make an even bigger bet on the portable machine in Year Two. Jack and his team delivered the numbers.

After the second year, Jack was promoted to group president, overseeing multiple divisions. In all, there were three group presidents, and Jack was clearly in the running to take over when Franz retired. Jack took Andre with him as group head of marketing and Danita moved up to run the division.

Jack's intuitive grasp of right fighting enabled him to deliver against a tough challenge. In the rest of the book, we explore the six Right Fight Principles in depth to help you face and surmount your organizational battles.

Part TWO

LEARN *to* PICK *the* RIGHT FIGHTS: *The* RIGHT FIGHT DECISION PRINCIPLES

FOUR

Right Fight Principle #1:
Make It Material

WRONG FIGHTS ARE just wrong. They're the reason people tend to avoid conflict whenever they can. All those meaningless battles over parking spaces, corner offices, and small variances in the numbers exhaust everyone involved and debilitate organizations.

So the first principle of a right fight is fundamental: *make it material*. What is at stake has got to matter. Right fights are about the big things, things that have the potential to change the performance and success of an organization and energize its people. No matter how conflict-avoidant they are in general, most people *are* willing to fight for things that will dramatically improve their well-being. And tension and fighting about things that don't really matter truly is a waste of time and energy. So make it material.

DOES IT MATTER?—THE VALUE TEST

So how do you tell if something is material? There are three basic tests. First, a successful outcome can create significant value for the organization. That value can come from any of a number of places, but three areas stand out when it comes to material value for a business entity: lasting cost advantage, a competitive difference that leads to premium prices or rapid market share growth, or a substantial reduction in risk.

The first two of these sources of value were confirmed by the McKinsey Global Institute almost a decade ago. Profiling dozens of companies that had grown from zero to $1 billion in revenues over a four-year period, the researchers could identify only two patterns of success. Successful companies either maintained a 20 percent cost advantage over their next best competitor for the whole time period, or—also over the whole four years—they achieved performance levels their competitors could not match on one of the top three attributes that led customers to chose one product or service over another. So, at least in the extreme case of explosive growth, the bar for material value is high.

The larger the organization, the more difficult it is to demonstrate this kind of explosive growth. If Wal-Mart or Exxon-Mobil maintained this kind of trajectory, they would absorb the entire global economy in a short period of time. Corporate giants need to look at the parts of their companies that are the next frontier of success—say, Wal-Mart's expansion into the

UK—and hold the pieces up to the materiality standard. And the larger and more complicated the organization, the more the third value lever comes into play—the reduction of risk. To understand the value of right fights that lower risk, all you have to do is think Enron, MCI WorldCom, Lehman Brothers, or Merrill Lynch.

So the first way to make a fight a right fight, to "make it material," is to make it about concrete value—real cost advantage, real differentiation from competition, or real reduction in risk.

DOES IT MATTER?—THE THINKING TEST

The second test of materiality has to do with the nature of the problem you're trying to solve. In her book *The Third Opinion*, Saj-nicole describes three types of thinking: application thinking, expert thinking, and exponential thinking. Application thinking is straightforward and involves known problems with routine solutions—for example, a machine on your production line breaks down, so you call maintenance to fix it. Expert thinking is more complex and requires specialized expertise—the machine keeps breaking, so you call in the manufacturer, they figure out that a specific part is wearing out too quickly, and they create a custom part for you. Neither of these types of problems is the domain of right fights. If the answer is routine, or specialized expertise is a phone call away, why would you waste the time and energy to fight about it?

It's the arena of exponential or out-of-the-box thinking that is likely to pass the materiality test and become the basis of a right fight. Let's suppose the machine keeps breaking even with the specialized part. What do you do now? The answer is to bring in many more perspectives and figure out what is systematically causing the machine to break. Is it being overused? Is there a way to lower demand on it so it stays up more of the time? Can you slow the entire line down and actually improve throughput because you don't have to deal with constant maintenance? Or is it the environment—what if you lowered the humidity or increased airflow?

When the value of combined insights from multiple perspectives is significantly greater than the sum of the individual points of view, you have the basis for a right fight. Interestingly enough, this is also Jon Katzenbach's (of Booz) classic definition of a "real team" performance challenge. Right fights require material trade-offs and innovative thinking from multiple parts of the organization. If your purchasing function can give you a lasting 20 percent cost advantage with minimal involvement from other parts of your business, there's no reason to fight at all. Give them the authority to cut costs and put the money in the bank. On the other hand, if a 20 percent cost advantage can come only from compromises and trade-offs in multiple areas that involve significant numbers of employees and impact customers and suppliers as well, you have the makings of a material right fight.

DOES IT MATTER?—THE CHANGE TEST

The third and final test of materiality has to do with lasting change. The result of a material fight should be a noticeable and sustainable difference in the way an organization works.

Consider the all-too-common problem of scale. The ways things work when a business is small usually become very hard to replicate when the business gets large, especially when size means the complexity of working across multiple countries and cultures, in multiple time zones, and across increasingly specialized organizational disciplines. In a start-up, a lot happens in the founder's head or in one-on-one conversations among a small group of people. Introduce departments, functions, and business units, and the natural integration that exists in a small organization can easily get lost. Too often, leaders mistake this loss of natural integration as some other problem entirely.

Take the example of Southwest Airlines in the aftermath of 9/11. Customer complaints were on the rise, and there were significant increases in delayed and lost bags. It was easy to point to the increased security requirements imposed on the travel industry as the root cause of the problems. But the reality was something much more subtle.

Southwest was becoming the victim of its own success. The once predominantly regional carrier was increasingly attracting customers who flew longer distances. A businessman traveling from Houston to Dallas for the day doesn't check a bag. And weather delays, though common, are relatively easy to recover from when the flight lasts an hour and you fly the route a dozen times a day. But a trip from Houston to New York is different. Longer hauls mean more checked baggage, and bad weather in New York can create delays that backlog flights for days.

Southwest's business had entered a new stage of complexity at the exact moment the shadow of terrorism changed the travel industry forever. The way the airline was used to working didn't suit the increased complexity of its business. When Southwest was tiny, its founder, Herb Kelleher, would literally call his best customers and let them know flights were delayed. But when the airline grew to over 500 planes, over 100 million passengers, and thousands of flights a day, that kind of personal troubleshooting wasn't possible anymore.

What happened instead is what always happens: deep specialization and systems. There were passenger systems, baggage systems, gate assignment systems, scheduling systems, and customer service systems—all function-specific and optimized for the piece of the puzzle they were designed to serve. The end-to-end passenger view got increasingly lost. Going back to the past wasn't an option, so the company brought in a team of high-powered consultants and IT specialists to rethink the way the company integrated all the things that had to happen, from the customer perspective. And over the course of eighteen months the company changed the way the different departments and systems worked with each other to manage the overall flight experience of its customers, instead of picking apart pieces of it. Service improved, complaints fell, and the airline was off to its next great growth adventure.

So to be material, a right fight has to create significant value, require integration of multiple perspectives, and change the way work gets done in an organization. In short, a material fight is worth the trouble.

MAKING IT MATTER—LIVE ON BROADWAY

On the face of it, a Broadway show may not look like a contender for a right fight that meets the materiality principle. Live theater is a relatively small industry in terms of revenue and broad-range social impact. Just over 12 million people attend Broadway shows each year, and the entire industry grosses less than $1 billion per year.

But for a fight to be material, it only has to matter to that particular organization, industry, or category of human activity. In the following case, Disney wanted to change the economics and the art of Broadway, and nothing less than a right fight would get the company there.

CASE STUDY: The Lion King *Reigns: Julie Taymor Directs a Hit for Disney*

- **The Value Test:** Disney expected a huge hit in a notoriously volatile market.
- **The Thinking Test:** Conventional methods couldn't turn an animated film into live theater.
- **The Change Test:** Could Taymor open new avenues for performance in a tradition-steeped field?

When Disney turned to Julie Taymor to direct a live theatrical version of its 1994 hit movie, *The Lion King*, the company was making a big bet on a relative newcomer. *The Lion King* still holds the record as the highest-grossing traditionally animated film of all time, and Disney planned to extend and protect the franchise in order to produce a huge moneymaker for a long time. Taymor had enjoyed some success directing theater and had developed a considerable reputation for innovative thinking, but she had no big-budget credits to point to, nor any standout Broadway hits.

Nonetheless, Taymor had unusually deep credentials as an expert in a highly specialized field. She had traveled the world studying folklore and had directed productions of several Shakespeare plays as well as a fairy tale, *The King Stag* (1984). Taymor had recently turned to the highly theatrical world of opera, staging a production of Igor Stravinsky's *Oedipus Rex* with Seiji Ozawa in Japan that earned an Emmy award in 1992.

So there was enormous pressure on her to succeed, and succeed big. Taymor herself had competing goals. The show had to be recognizable as the Disney classic, of course, but she also wanted the production to evoke the spirit of Africa and her own unmistakable style. Add to this list the expectation that the play would be a commercial success and her understandable personal desire for critical acclaim and you have a very tall order indeed.

Creating a show like *The Lion King* wasn't easy. Taymor had to mix traditional theater, innovative elements, and quintessential Disney in equal measure. And she had to do it all on a strict timetable and within a tight budget in a theatrical world where cost overruns and production delays are all too common.

Taymor's solution was to bring in a team that was an eclectic mix of designers and musicians—and a choreographer—few of whom had extensive Broadway experience before working on *The Lion King*. Not being limited to conventional wisdom about how a musical is done, the composers, choreographer, designers, and performers were able to draw on all sorts of different ideas and disciplines to solve the myriad creative problems that arose during the designing, staging, and rehearsing of the elaborate musical.

For example, while there are over half a dozen schools of puppetry represented in the show, none of the actors was an experienced puppeteer. The lack of seasoned experience meant that tensions ran high during the two years of workshops that it took to bring the show to the stage. But the fights the team were fighting were the right ones. Taymor kept things focused on her unique vision to integrate Broadway, puppetry, and Disney in a way that would transform the theatrical experience for the audience. From the award-winning costumes that allow the audience to see actor and animal at the same time to the African rhythms that purposely collide with Elton John's pop tunes, Taymor creatively managed tensions between the artistic and the practical, between budget and design, between choreography, music, visuals, and book.

In the end, the show was an extraordinarily successful fusion of tradition and originality. Opened in July 1997, it is still going strong. Its London production opened in 1999 and is still playing to sold-out houses. The show has traveled the world and seen productions in Japan, China, Canada, Australia, Korea, Holland, France, and South Africa. The original show won six Tony Awards, including two for Taymor, making her the first woman to win a Tony for direction of a musical.

The Lion King is an incredibly rare combination of critical and commercial success because Taymor instinctively "made it material" in staging the show. As Taymor's example shows, however, making it matter doesn't make it easy. When a right fight is material to an organization's success, tensions that cause conflict don't go away and they aren't ignored. Instead, like Taymor directing *The Lion King*, leaders must manage these tensions productively in ways that create value, exploit exponential thinking, and support lasting improvements in organizational behavior and performance.

MAKING IT MATTER— WORKING ON THE RAILROAD

In inherently creative projects like *The Lion King*, the people involved probably expect both visionary leadership and a certain amount of clashing between differing artistic viewpoints. Managing the right fights over what matters in creative disciplines like theater is part and parcel of the leader's job, because standards of evaluation are subjective. But the need to orchestrate right fights that are material is just as critical to organizational success in more pragmatic and conventional businesses, where what's at stake is absolutely concrete and objectively quantifiable.

CASE STUDY: *Burlington Northern Makes Tracks: Charlie Feld Alters the Landscape for Railroads*

- **The Value Test:** BN wanted to grab a slice of the global intermodal shipping market.
- **The Thinking Test:** Nineteenth-century methods weren't up to the challenges of twenty-first-century logistics.
- **The Change Test:** Could Feld get everyone to think big and see what was possible?

When Charlie Feld decided to form The Feld Group, he had big aspirations. Formerly a highly successful CIO at Frito-Lay, Feld sought to transform the IT profession and develop a new generation of "chief integration officers." Not your typical CIO, Feld possesses two rare abilities that almost never come together in a single IT leader: he understands the opportunities and limitations of specific technologies, and he can sell his vision in boardrooms. In his first assignment after Frito-Lay he needed to do both equally well.

Coming to Burlington Northern in the mid-1990s, Feld was amazed at what he found. "I used to be able to tell you where every bag of Doritos was in the country and they lost *locomotives*. How is that possible? They're big, smelly, and they sit on a track with only a limited number of places where they can go." With typical humor, Feld immediately put his finger on one of the key problems facing the business. The physical railroad and the electronic railroad were never in sync. BN was running trains using processes and systems designed for an era of hauling coal and grain. It didn't make much difference to the coal or the corn whether the train showed up on Monday or a week from Monday.

But Jerry Grinstein, then chairman and CEO of BN, had a much bigger vision in mind. Grinstein wanted to expand the intermodal business and take back market share lost to truckers over decades. Knowing that the U.S. economy was going to rely increasingly on imports for everything from steel to automobiles, Grinstein planned to transition BN into the "gateway for Asia."

The opportunity was as huge as the challenges. The cost advantages of rail were material by anyone's definition, but running a "scheduled railroad" was no easy trick. As with most large organizations, BN was a series of silos. In order to schedule a shipment of multiple commodities, a customer had to call the grain desk and the coal desk, get separate price quotes, call separate dispatch lines to actually schedule transport, then deal with separate customer service departments if issues arose. While coal and grain shippers didn't really have other viable options, the difficulty of navigating the BN system wasn't likely to woo intermodal shippers.

The systems that supported operations were just as difficult to navigate internally. Price quotes were created from huge loose-leaf binders. Different departments had different technologies, and IT systems didn't talk to one another. As a result BN couldn't create customer-specific strategic pricing or get its act together on much of anything else.

And even worse, no one knew where the trains were at any given time. Trainmasters in depots throughout the country ran the railroad blind, able to react only when a train actually entered their station, unable to plan ahead or respond to unexpected events. It took the railroad weeks if not months to recover from rainstorms that damaged track or took out bridges. If BN was going to become the gateway for a whole new generation of shippers, the railroad was going to have to run in a fundamentally different way.

Feld brought in a high-powered team of IT professionals who, while having very little railroad experience, had built state-of-the-art integrated customer service, pricing, and logistics systems. The team mapped out the technical challenges in a ninety-day diagnostic that clearly contrasted an objective view of the current state of operations with a future vision of what was possible for an effectively scheduled railroad.

Feld presented his case to the board. They approved his plan to spend more than $100 million over eighteen months to build the new systems. The plan was not a painless one and not without conflict: Feld replaced 100 of the top 150 IT leaders within his first ninety days on the job.

But according to Feld, the hardest part wasn't laying people off or figuring out how to tie the archaic legacy systems together into a unified, real-time electronic structure. Although there were significant technical challenges involved, the real challenge wasn't technical at all. It was convincing all the functional departments to embrace a new way of working. Running a tighter railroad meant changing the way things had been done for over a hundred years. Instead of a loosely self-managed network of local train stations, the new BN would be centrally run out of corporate headquarters on the edge of downtown Fort Worth.

While Feld was a master at painting a compelling future vision, he knew that to get people to embrace the tough operating changes that were in store, there had to be a real gap between their perception of BN's current state of operations and the ideal state of end-to-end integration he envisioned. "If people don't rate today somewhere between a two and a four, and tomorrow somewhere between a seven and a nine, they'll never embrace the changes that have to happen," Feld says.

On the operations side, Feld was fortunate to work with a long-time friend and colleague from his Frito-Lay days, Ron Rittenmeyer. Rittenmeyer had been hired by Grinstein to run BN operations around the same time Feld was brought in to revamp IT. Ron was the epitome of a turnaround guy: tough-minded, relentless, and keenly focused on performance. If anyone at BN felt that the current state wasn't so bad, Rittenmeyer could quickly convince them otherwise. Together they pulled together teams from operations, marketing, sales, customer service, and IT to map out what the new systems and ways of working would have to look and feel like.

Knowing that people couldn't embrace systems they were unable even to imagine, Feld knew he had to show BN leaders what was possible. Feld and Rittemeyer hosted a boardroom pilot where the new systems and capabilities were put on display. A customer call automatically triggered output of integrated sales, pricing, and logistics information, allowing reps to give their accounts real-time status of shipments, payments, and quotes. Dispatchers could view trains and their locations alongside weather forecasts, commodity prices, and closed-circuit images of switching locations. It was like going from a soap-box derby to mission control at NASA.

Ultimately, the new systems were delivered on time and under budget. A merger with Santa Fe in 1995, and the associated departure of Grinstein and Rittenmeyer, created a temporary setback for the timeline, but Robert Krebs, incoming chair and chief executive of the combined entity, was a consummate operator himself, and fully embraced the changes Feld and Rittemeyer were putting into place.

If you visit BNSF today, more than a decade later, you will find the fundamental architecture of the scheduled railroad alive and well. GPS trackers on railcars allow the dispatchers in Fort Worth to pinpoint not only where trains are, but in what direction and at what rate of speed they are moving. BNSF's intermodal business is large, profitable, growing, and continuing to gain share from truckers in everything from UPS shipments at Christmas to cars off Toyota's Asian assembly lines. The new way of working has fundamentally repositioned BNSF against its nearest competitor, the Union Pacific Railroad. From nearly identical starting points in 2004, BNSF's stock price has more than tripled, and is currently twice that of UP's.

By all definitions of materiality—value, vision, and viable change—Feld clearly picked a right fight in building a scheduled railroad. Although the process was long, the challenges great, and the conflicts many, Feld made it material and as a result Burlington Northern came out on top.

FIVE

Right Fight Principle #2: Focus on the Future, Not the Past

LIKE CHARLIE FELD at Burlington Northern, leaders in viable, vibrant organizations spend most of their time and energy focused on the future. They recognize that those with a backward view miss opportunities in the here and now, and they understand that attention to the present moment becomes increasingly important in this global electronic age. Market shifts now occur more rapidly and frequently than ever, demanding equally speedy response and much agility on the ground.

From the standpoint of the materiality principle, a vision for the future of an organization looks like an ideal candidate for a right fight. In most cases, this is true. And the more the debate includes a willingness to look at extreme possibilities as well as likelier scenarios, the more productive it's likely to be.

Focusing on the future, though, is much easier to say than it is in practice to do. Given that everyone knows the past can't be changed, it's amazing how much time people in most organizations spend arguing about it. In our work with senior leadership teams around the globe, we track how much of the conversation revolves around what's over and done.

Typically, leadership teams spend 85 percent of their time together sorting out the numbers, trying to figure out what went wrong or dissecting what went well, assigning blame or recognition—and *all* of these conversations are discussions centered in the past. Essentially, most teams are wasting time, energy, and brainpower when they could be investing their resources wisely toward future returns. Obsession with past performance, or intense interest in decisions made months or even years before, is a dead giveaway that your organization is stuck in a wrong fight.

THE FUTURE IS A MOVING TARGET

There are risks, though, in taking on a fight about the future. For one thing, it's very easy to keep on fighting once the future has become the past. Organizations should always be ready to move on. Once a right fight is fought and finished, you need to drop the tensions quickly. Postmortem reviews have value only to the extent that they yield important insights about changing behavior in the future. Figure out what you've learned from the particular experiment and how you're going to apply those lessons to the next issue. But do it fast and get on to the next challenge.

You also need to examine the future you're focused on.

Organizations that aren't self-aware tend to make the same mistakes over and over again. The U.S. auto industry is a classic example of a business continuing into the future on a path that leaders had every reason to know was unsustainable, hoping they would not have to change as the world around them changed. Ultimately, in 2009, this led to government bailouts, widespread layoffs, bankruptcy, and the dismantling of a hallmark U.S. industry. It's not enough to learn how to do what you're doing better and better—you need to challenge basic assumptions about your business and about what the future looks like, or you'll just get better and better at doing the *wrong* things.

FUTURE FOCUS IS LEADER DRIVEN

As the auto industry example shows, true future focus requires people to change their habitual ways of working. Projecting into the future demands the kind of exponential, integrative thinking that makes a fight material. It takes skillful leadership to manage the process and promote positive outcomes.

Leadership development is a function usually buried in HR, but is often far more important to right fights than performance management. Although this may sound counterintuitive, remember how much time most teams spend talking about the past. It is the leader's role to redirect the conversation. Attaining a desirable future depends heavily on her skill in focusing tensions productively on a future worth fighting for.

Several years ago, the pharmaceutical firm Pfizer realized

that it was taking fifteen years or more to promote leaders in its finance division to the level of vice president. Pfizer had finance directors who were excellent analysts, but who were not viewed as trusted business advisors. The CFO realized that it was no longer enough for finance professionals to leverage their technical and quantitative abilities in better systems. Business leaders up and down the organization were looking to them to provide "second opinions" on a variety of options. To unlock performance, he needed better leaders.

The CFO announced his intent to accelerate the development of business acumen in the finance organization. Conventional wisdom said that he had competing priorities because he wanted finance directors with deep specialized financial expertise, strong interpersonal skills, *and* sound business insight, but the CFO was determined to create a new generation of finance professionals.

Working with us and the company head of internal learning, the finance leadership created a multifaceted training program. The pressure was intense. Participants had to work with their peers, some of whom they had competed against for promotion, in small teams, on a complex real-life pricing problem. They had to generate multiple possible answers and defend them to the CFO, giving each other intense developmental feedback along the way.

Results were dramatic. Significant numbers of promotions followed. One VP of finance commented, "The progress these people have made to change from 'number crunchers' into true thought partners to the business—in just a week—is simply astounding."

Pfizer created a deep pool of qualified leadership talent in a far shorter timeframe than most people in the organization thought possible. And that leadership talent had been specifically trained in a highly particular skill set. Faced with a challenging set of circumstances, they learned how to see past the present reality to a better possible future.

FUTURE FOCUS—THE POSSIBILITY TEST

Right fights about the future always speak to what is *possible*, not to what is past. Though it's important to understand why the past is what it is, there is rarely value in debating it. In fact, such debates are often the most frustrating part of organizational life. Empirical questions get revisited time and time again so individuals can add spin, color, and nuance—or worse, blame each other for wrong assumptions about what should have been done and wasn't.

But no matter who did what to whom or how the current numbers came to be, the truth is that no amount of discussion can change the facts. Debates of fact are important and they have their place. Our legal system is predicated on them. But debates about *what to do about the facts* are far more interesting and productive. Beyond blame and accountability, there is the excitement of possibility.

Right fights move beyond the blame game to focus on what is possible and to make what is possible actually happen. When leadership teams hold interesting, effective, high-quality conversations about the future, their discussions exhibit a predictable but not chronological timeline. These discussions begin in the past, not to assign blame but to recover information. They next jump to the future as the team explores vision or possibility. Only then does the conversation move into the present as team members request specific actions and secure additional commitments. It's a sure sign of trouble if this past-future-present sequence is violated.

The most common violation occurs when leaders go from the past to the present without setting the context of a future worth having. "We missed the numbers this quarter so we're going to cut our costs to make up our margins," the vice president declares. Such past-to-present logic is all too pervasive in leaders. Too often, it leads to blame-fests and creates performance death spirals that make future recovery all but impossible to accomplish. It would be far more productive for the VP to structure a right fight around achieving short-term results that are good enough while deploying resources toward the possibility of long-term success.

FUTURE FOCUS—THE COMPELLING TEST

But changing the flow of debate from blame for the past to possibility in the future is only the first step. For a right fight about the future to be worth fighting, there has to be a significant gap between today's reality and the future vision. That's why right fights about the future are almost always about innovation and breakthrough performance—

the possibility at stake needs to be big enough that people will come together to do something collectively that they cannot do alone.

Again, as Charlie Feld argues, if people can't imagine a future state that is significantly better than what they experience today, it's nearly impossible to get them to change.

The possibilities inherent in change are most attractive to people who see themselves stuck at low but not abysmal levels of satisfaction, levels where the need for change is clear but the scary scenario of a full slash-and-burn turnaround campaign isn't likely. It's the contrast between the two-to-four real present and the seven-to-nine possible future that is motivating. A smaller gap makes it hard for leadership to move people out of the box and toward the nonlinear thinking required to create the future.

So if visionary leaders want a productive right fight to help them get to a possible future, they have to make the future vision not only believable and desirable but compelling—so compelling, in fact, that *not* making it happen becomes the problem. Change is never easy and big change usually entails some big issues and headaches. A truly compelling future vision focuses people so intently on real, achievable benefits that they are willing to work through the costs and controversies associated with achieving those benefits.

Compelling future visions are worth right fights.

FUTURE FOCUS—THE UNCERTAINTY TEST

The third and final characteristic required for a right fight about the future is uncertainty. If how to get to the future is clear and people still bicker over the process, that's a sure sign of a wrong fight. Such wrong fights occur for lots of different reasons—lack of personal or expertise trust in the people in charge, desire for personal gain, or stubborn reliance on archaic methods or outdated thinking—but they need to be recognized and defused.

Where there isn't uncertainty, there's no reason to argue. And the future is not always shrouded in mist. Compaq computer's meteoric rise to the Fortune 500 and then the Fortune 100 in the mid-1990s was driven not by right fights predicated on uncertainty but by exploiting obvious opportunities in the market. In 1991, the newly appointed CEO, Eckhard Pfeiffer, set the company on two strategic paths. First he declared a price war and created tremendous internal pressure on costs, ultimately reducing prices by 30 percent in a single year. The once-small brand known for innovation was immediately repositioned against IBM as a value player. Although there was uncertainty as to where the cost reductions would come from, Pfeiffer's team knew they could take advantage of technology cost-curve declines to make the numbers work.

The second element of Pfeiffer's strategy involved geography. From a solid sales base in the United States, Pfeiffer opened sales offices at the rate of more than one country per month for two years, swiftly penetrating untapped personal computing markets in Europe and Asia. Both of these moves were material and both were focused on the future, but neither required a right fight. The strategic path was clear and there was no real need for debate.

Right fights demand real uncertainty, and that uncertainty needs to be managed with sensitivity, acumen, and close attention. So when is the future uncertain enough to be worth a right fight? Two situations come to mind.

The first situation occurs when the external environment is so unstable that a definitive path forward is difficult to see. Lots of things can cause this kind of strategic uncertainty: changes in policy or regulation, an economic downturn or boom, unexpected changes in customer preferences, disruptive technologies. Uncertainty tools like scenario planning can be very useful in staging right fights when the external environment is in flux. Scenario planning involves the intentional invention of various plausible, internally consistent end states to test the outcomes of different actions. In a right fight, each scenario about how the future is likely to unfold has an internal advocate who argues for it with passion, judgment, and a healthy degree of expected self-interest.

The second situation is when the external environment is fairly clear but potentially threatening, and the best way forward is far from certain. Like our fictionalized protagonist, Jack Sparr, leaders are often faced with high-stakes options in circumstances that don't yield obvious decision markers. Here the value of a right fight is in clarifying the real trade-offs and actual costs of different choices so leaders can pick the best alternative.

FUTURE FOCUS—DO THE DEAL?

A leader who keeps his organization looking forward is a tremendous asset. Promoting possibility, creating a compelling vision, and resolving uncertainty in positive and equitable ways will yield marked improvements in both organizational outcomes and individual levels of satisfaction. So how does a future-focused leader act? What are his priorities? What things does he think are worth fighting for?

CASE STUDY: *To Buy or Not to Buy? New CEO Rolf Classon Referees Competing Visions*

- **The Possibility Test:** Two potential futures painted competing pictures of what could be.
- **The Compelling Test:** Each option promised change, but in differing measures and in different directions.
- **The Uncertainty Test:** The environment was unpredictable, but could Classon hold the debate open long enough in the face of organizational demands for closure?

Rolf Classon moved up into the role of CEO and immediately found himself in a controversy that would significantly affect the future of a $48 billion company. How would he make the right choice? A misstep early in his tenure could seriously limit his ability to lead, perhaps even jeopardize his tenure as CEO. The stakes were very high, way beyond the money, resources, and people involved.

The company was seriously considering a sizable acquisition in a sector where they already had a smaller presence. The deal had been vetted and set in motion by the former CEO and his leadership team. Together with the company's own moderately sized business, the new, much bigger entity would be capable of dominating the industry. But in Classon's first few weeks on the job, a colleague stepped forward in private and told Classon that while there was considerable momentum for the deal, he was unsure it was the right move, and it was keeping him up at night.

Classon recognized the courage of his colleague's honesty, so he decided to take another look at the proposed acquisition. There were a number of challenges in opening the inquiry. Could he make it clear that he was looking for a genuine answer, not just ratification of existing opinion? Could he avoid alienating the executives who had championed the acquisition? Could he stop a deal that had so much momentum behind it? Carefully, Classon took the first steps toward a right fight to decide the merits of the acquisition. He asked a few other executives for their thoughts. When he found that some also had private doubts, Classon knew he had to act.

So Classon went to the chairman, and told him he needed to review the deal before pulling the trigger. The board supported his request and Classon set a strategic right fight in motion. He recalls, "It was a loud debate, a spirited discussion involving about ten executives who had very strong views on the subject. It was a long, tense several weeks. We did studies, had arguments, and brought in outside experts."

The division head who would have integrated the acquisition was, at first, furious. The acquisition meant a great deal to his career, and he'd been working on it for a long time. Classon took great care to give the division head not only a voice in the fight but also access to the board, essentially giving permission for him to go around the usual hierarchy so that all views were fully heard.

Classon asked the team to look at the deal's feasibility as well as its alignment with the company's strategic objectives. To ensure a right fight, Classon made it a point to be a scrupulously fair referee. He did not hire consultants to prove his point; in fact, he went to great lengths to ensure their studies were independent. His team tested him, trying to see if his mind was made up. It was not. He wanted to hear everyone's views, and he made it safe to air them.

The debate revealed differences of opinion about the likely performance of the combined new business. The numbers were strong but the business was tricky, with a cyclical demand and complex regulatory issues. But in the end, despite likely positive financial results, the firm decided not to pursue the deal, because leadership came together and agreed that there was more strategic advantage in shifting their overall business portfolio toward consumer segments of the market.

Classon staged a right fight over his company's future, and he managed it brilliantly. He kept his team focused on future possibilities, in spite of the pressure to cling to a decision made in the past. He encouraged people to engage in authentic debate about those possibilities by soliciting lots of viewpoints and giving everyone a fair hearing. He even managed to hang on to the executive who was to head up the new division by asking him to lead another major division—an assignment that made it clear that Classon valued and respected him and that stopping the deal was not a vote of no confidence.

In addition to keeping focus on the future, Classon structured the debate to produce a compelling future vision that energized people to fight for it. The acquisition didn't significantly move forward the intended strategic direction of the company, and Classon's inquiry forced the organization to rethink and retest its commitment to this strategy at a crucial moment. The right fight kept the firm from making a costly mistake and brought focus back to its strategic identity as a consumer-driven company.

Finally, Classon worked the whole process in the context of real and consequential uncertainty. He was a new CEO, he didn't know the territory intimately, and he had only weeks to research and decide something vital to the future of the organization he had just stepped up to lead. What enabled his success was his genuine curiosity, his commitment to open and dissonant dialogue, his patient focus on building strategic intent into sustainable reality, and his skill in orchestrating a right fight that mattered.

FUTURE FOCUS—WATCHING THE WALL

They say politics is the art of the possible, and politicians, to a far greater extent than CEOs, achieve their success by painting compelling visions of the future that sway people their way. So it might seem that right fights would rule the day in politics. But given the disparate interests and competing agendas in political arenas, political right fights are notoriously hard to pull off.

CASE STUDY: *The Oval Office in the Cold War: President Reagan Manages His Speechwriters*

- **The Possibility Test:** Reagan's team was polarized by politics, but firmly focused on the shape of things to come.
- **The Compelling Test:** The defeat of Communism. Enough said.
- **The Uncertainty Test:** At an insecure moment in international relations, how far could Reagan challenge Gorbachev? How would the world react?

President Ronald Reagan surrounded himself with moderate staffers in his second term—men like Colin Powell, then in the National Security Council, Chief of Staff Howard Baker, and Secretary of State George Shultz. His speechwriting staff, however, continued to be keepers of the right-wing flame. There were many speechwriters—the turnover rate was very high—but among the second-termers who were considered doctrinally pure were Josh Gilder, Peggy Noonan, and Peter Robinson.

There was much press speculation at the time that the moderate new staffers were holding the president back, not allowing "Reagan to be Reagan" and watering down the strong, pure words of the speechwriting team so much that by the time Reagan actually delivered his speeches, they no longer said what he really wanted to say. True believers argued that if unadulterated 200 proof Reagan was uncorked by the speechwriters and poured into the speeches, the president's popularity would improve, the country would shake itself free of its doldrums, and Communism would find itself permanently on the defensive.

The speechwriters fed this line of argument by leaking tales of their struggles to the press. They whispered that they had written great, blistering, doctrinaire anti-Communist rhetoric, only to have it watered down by those pusillanimous middle-of-the-roaders at State before Reagan ever saw it. Indeed, the net effect of these stories in the press was to support the growing view in the country that Reagan was a disengaged, aging president being manipulated by his staff.

The press stories, though, significantly misrepresented what was actually going on behind the scenes. Reagan's famous 1987 speech at the Brandenburg Gate in West Berlin is a case in point. Historian Robert Schlesinger sets the scene in his book *White House Ghosts: Presidents and Their Speechwriters* (Simon & Schuster, 2008):

The United States and Soviet Union had made lurching progress toward détente in the mid-1980s. Reagan met Mikhail Gorbachev at the Vienna summit in late 1985, which was viewed as a success. The summit at Reykjavik in 1986, however, was seen as a failure after Reagan broke off talks over his cherished anti-missile system. But negotiations were moving forward over an Intermediate Nuclear Forces treaty, and, more broadly, Gorbachev was starting to push reforms of the Soviet system.

Speechwriter Robinson went to West Berlin ahead of the presidential entourage to research the situation and gather material for the speech Reagan planned to give at the historic Brandenburg Gate. The gate speech was just one event in a European tour designed, in part, to shore up Reagan's reputation at home by showcasing his interaction with other world leaders.

Robinson met first with the top U.S. diplomat in West Berlin, John Kornblum. Kornblum was very concerned that Reagan not ruffle any German or Communist feathers, and he gave Robinson a long list of things the president should not say—nothing angry or aggressive, nothing about the Wall; nothing, in short, that anyone would remember.

Robinson then had dinner with a local family and a group of their friends to get a sense of what the mood was like on the ground. Basically the West Berliners were blasé about their situation and uninterested in East-West tension. But when Robinson asked them specifically about the Wall, something surprising happened. People at the dinner had impassioned stories to tell about families divided, people they could see but never meet, and so on. One man told of passing the same East German guard standing on the Wall as he went to work each morning. The man said, "That soldier and I speak the same language. We share the same history. But one of us is a zookeeper and the other is an animal, and I am never certain which is which." At the end of the evening, the hostess, a retired woman, pounded her fist and exclaimed, "If this man Gorbachev is serious with his talk of glasnost and perestroika, he can get rid of this Wall."

Robinson could see right away that he had touched a nerve and he focused his theme for the speech on tearing down the Wall. The speech went through many drafts, with the crucial phrase "Mr. Gorbachev, tear down this Wall!" evolving, first in German, then in English.

The speechwriting staff knew they had a potentially incendiary line. They plotted strategies carefully to ensure that it would survive the review process so that Reagan might actually utter the words. In the end, they placed the speech at the bottom of the pile of speeches the president would deliver on the nine-day trip, and presented it to him for weekend reading only a week before his departure.

The speechwriters met with Reagan on Monday. As it happened, the one line Reagan noted from the Robinson speech was the remark about tearing down the Wall, and that gave Robinson and the others the ammunition they needed to fight for it. The National Security Council, the State Department, and Kornblum argued forcefully that confronting Gorbachev on the Wall risked slowing the progress of détente. Baker,

Shultz, and Powell all weighed in, recommending that the line be removed.

But Reagan had decided to deliver the line, and it stayed. Thus, on June 12, 1987, Reagan voiced one of the most famous lines of his presidency in a speech which was vintage anti-Communist, pro-freedom Reagan:

> And now the Soviets themselves may, in a limited way, be coming to understand the importance of freedom. We hear much from Moscow about a new policy of reform and openness. Some political prisoners have been released. Certain foreign news broadcasts are no longer being jammed. Some economic enterprises have been permitted to operate with greater freedom from state control.
>
> Are these the beginnings of profound changes in the Soviet state? Or are they token gestures, intended to raise false hopes in the West, or to strengthen the Soviet system without changing it? We welcome change and openness; for we believe that freedom and security go together, that the advance of human liberty can only strengthen the cause of world peace. There is one sign the Soviets can make that would be unmistakable, that would advance dramatically the cause of freedom and peace.
>
> General Secretary Gorbachev, if you seek peace, if you seek prosperity for the Soviet Union and Eastern Europe, if you seek liberalization: Come here to this gate! Mr. Gorbachev, open this gate! Mr. Gorbachev, tear down this wall!

The press version of the story had things backward. This was not a case of Reagan being handled by factions on a polarized staff. Nor did the speechwriters put words in the president's mouth. Reagan had a history of speeches going back some thirty years—from his tenure as spokesman for General Electric, his terms as governor of California, and his presidential campaigns—so it was easy for staffers to access and represent his views on most subjects. The truth was that Reagan intentionally pitted the moderates on his staff against the doctrinaire conservatives so that on virtually every issue he heard at least two sides argued with conviction before he made up his mind. Reagan was orchestrating a right fight about the future of democracy and Communism, and he was referee.

History still debates whether or not Reagan was an *effective* referee, and that debate is likely to continue. By all accounts, Reagan was a notoriously hands-off manager, and the White House is at the best of times an unrelenting, unforgiving, exhausting place to work—the players involved are powerful, the bureaucracy complicated, and the issues huge.

But Reagan's fight was a right one. It mattered—a lot—and in spite of enormous unknowns he focused it single-mindedly on a compelling future vision of freedom and possibility. Right fights are not always tidy. But they are always worth the struggle.

SIX

Right Fight Principle #3: Pursue a Noble Purpose

ALL GREAT ORGANIZATIONS are mission driven in the sense that they are focused on something bigger than who's in charge of what. It is fundamentally important for the forward momentum of any organization to ask itself, on a regular basis, *what's our purpose?* If that purpose is not somehow useful to the world, the organization will eventually die, so the question needs to be real and pointed.

At a fundamental level, in order for a fight to be a right fight, it needs to be connected to this noble purpose. That's what makes the game worth the candle, because organizational development depends on organizational purpose. It might be easier at times not to serve the noble purpose, and to find other ways to solve organizational riddles. But right fights and noble purpose must be inextricably linked if an organization is to excel at serving all its stakeholders—customers, communities, people, shareholders.

IT'S NOT JUST ABOUT THE MONEY

In the business world, it's often assumed that the creation of shareholder value is in itself every enterprise's primary and all-sufficient purpose. While investors can legitimately take that point of view, savvy investors rarely do. Even the most financially driven stakeholder will want to know at some point what makes the organization he invests in tick, what drives its ordinary people to deliver above average results. And the answer to that question almost never lies solely in financial performance.

Remember Doug Conant's turnaround at Campbell? Short-sighted focus on financial performance at the expense of important intangibles—like innovation and quality—had driven a cascade of bad decisions and had led the company to near financial ruin before Conant became CEO. Conant's answer was not only to rebalance long-term and short-term thinking. It was to restore the organization's sense of purpose in nourishing people's lives.

PURSUING PURPOSE—
THE INTANGIBILITY TEST

A noble purpose has to be about more than making money. It sometimes surprises leaders to learn that at the heart of some of the most financially successful organizations are highly motivating but financially intangible statements of purpose.

It's hard to imagine an organization more ruthlessly focused on cost and efficiency than Wal-Mart. Frugality is a core value of the organization. Executives are expected to share hotel rooms when they travel.

The retail giant's world headquarters is an unassuming building in Bentonville, Arkansas, and ought to be a must-see tour stop for any serious student of thrift. Suppliers wait all day in uncomfortable plastic chairs in the lobby for brutal price negotiations with buyers. There are a couple of receptionists at a simple desk, and a few years ago, when we visited, you could buy a Coke for fifty cents or a Sam's cola for a quarter. The executive offices are small—seating three or four people at a time—and the bathrooms are off the front lobby.

Legend has it that, when Sam Walton was still alive, several leaders asked for an executive washroom to be installed to save senior executives the discomfort of passing anxious vendors in the lobby every time they had to go to the bathroom. Walton had a portable toilet delivered the next day, placed it prominently in the middle of the executive offices, and announced that anyone who was too good to walk to the common facilities could relieve himself in the new executive washroom. Walton made his point. While Wal-Mart shareholders and executives have attained a level of wealth beyond most of their dreams, there is still no executive washroom.

So what makes the giant continue to wage the right fight for lower prices? Miserly greed? The creation of even more shareholder wealth? If you ask anyone from the most senior executives to the average store employee what the company is about, you will likely hear some variation of "making living affordable for everyday people."

Wal-Mart's business practices have often been criticized. The company has driven mom-and-pop stores out of business and has permanently changed the landscape of small-town American retail. But at the heart of what they are doing is the belief that average folks should be able to buy the things they need to run their households at the best prices possible. Ruthless efficiency is the means to an end. This value has transcended changes in leadership, unprecedented growth, and now global expansion.

PURSUING PURPOSE—THE ENERGIZING TEST

While senior executives live in a world where earnings per share and value creation are motivating and by necessity the subject of many conversations, the average employee does not. How many times have you overheard someone talking about her job in terms of margins or earnings at a kids' soccer game? For most people, talking about the job means describing either what they do or how they feel about what they do.

A sense of noble purpose energizes people; it motivates them to go above and beyond in order to fulfill the purpose and achieve the goals it creates. For a fight to be right it needs to be about the purpose, and for the purpose to be worth fighting for there needs to be significant investment in that purpose at *all* levels of the organization, from senior executives down to hourly workers on the line.

It's important not to rush the process. Investment in purpose takes time—sometimes a lot of time. Doug Conant took six months to restate the vision, values, and purpose at Campbell not because he didn't know what the purpose was but because he wanted to maximize the benefits of getting everyone fully invested in it, energized by it, and willing to fight for it. Efficiency and speed are not always the best way to an answer even when the answer is clear.

Several years ago we did a pro bono project for the Katy Independent School District on the outskirts of Houston. Katy is a high-growth suburb largely because of its exemplary public schools. School funding in Texas is a complicated subject, but the basic economics work to the disadvantage of high-growth districts. Such districts have to raise money by getting voters to tax themselves, passing bonds to build facilities for kids whose parents haven't even moved into the area yet.

Although most people appreciate increasing property values when it comes time to sell their homes, they don't like paying bigger property tax bills every year. So while the majority of the community rallied around good schools as a clearly noble purpose, getting the bond approved was a very different issue.

The district had grown sizable enough that individual neighborhood interests began to overtake the larger interests of the district as a whole. The first bond package submitted to voters contained funds to build new schools, invest in technology, and repair some of the oldest schools in the system. At the grassroots level, it was hard to explain why bond money had to be paid now to build schools in five years. Teachers questioned the need for technology dollars to create an automated curriculum system—and teachers were the largest voting bloc in the district. Older neighborhoods jockeyed for larger shares of the renovation funding. There was also organized resistance from a small but vocal group of local citizens against public school funding. The bond proposal failed in a very close low-turnout election.

The superintendent at the time, Dr. Leonard Merrell, didn't take no for an answer. Failure meant the district would be dangerously close to dipping into its operating budget to pay for growth. Failure meant thousands of kids would have to go to school in temporary buildings, raising issues of equality and safety that no one in district administration wanted to have to deal with. It was time for a right fight.

Working with a group of dedicated community leaders appointed to form the bond committee, Dr. Merrell launched a textbook case of consensus-building for the next election. He brought together about 100 community leaders, parents, bond opponents, teachers, and a few representatives from his administration in a series of meetings to construct a new bond package.

Everyone worked from the same comprehensive data. In small groups they were asked to assemble a proposal that they could live with. The small groups created eight different proposals. Then they were combined into four larger groups and each group had to create a compromise proposal from the two incoming points of view. That led to another combination and ultimately a single proposal was created. Different neighborhoods' interests were heard, opponents were heard, and teachers soundly defeated the inclusion of technology. But everyone had to engage in the give-and-take that was required to come up with a feasible proposal. It took months, but the process invigorated the entire community and in the end the compromise proposal passed by a wide margin.

PURSUING PURPOSE—THE RESPECT TEST

Just like the community volunteers who crafted the Katy bond, the employees that leaders must motivate to fight the right fights need to care about what they're doing. And like the Katy bond committee, most employees care about doing things that their friends and neighbors will value and approve. If a fight can't be explained so that the average person understands it's a good thing to do, it's not likely to be a right fight.

When Betsy Myers was asked by President Bill Clinton to set up the Office for Women's Initiatives and Outreach—coordinating all activities of the administration focused on women, and getting the word out about what had been achieved—she understood her noble purpose well. It was the logistics that were problematic.

As a member of Clinton's team, Myers was entitled to office space in the West Wing, but the space available was tiny, cramped, and hard to get to. Being "inside the gate" was important in two different dimensions. First, Myers needed to coordinate across many initiatives and offices, and insider status would facilitate getting things done. Even more important, her direct personal access to the information loop would make all the difference in what her office could accomplish. To work in the West Wing is to play in a very high-stakes game. If you're outside, no one holds a place for you at the table.

But Myers also knew that for her office to be successful, it had to be accessible to women, and it had to create community and opportunities to listen. There was a great space right outside the gate—a two-story townhouse—and against the advice of many Myers decided to locate there. The solution wasn't perfect, but the location Myers chose hit the mark with her real constituency.

Women came from all over. They volunteered. They talked. They created. They got the word out to others. The location of the office revealed, in a literal and very powerful way, that Myers and her staff were primarily focused on people and issues outside the usual DC circles of influence. Myers and her team won the respect and commitment of those they served in a way that energized volunteers, petitioners, and leadership alike.

Defying conventional wisdom, Myers remained a powerful and very productive player, credited with a major role in delivering the women's vote that was essential in Clinton's reelection. She fought the right fight—retaining access even though she was outside the magic circle of the West Wing—by systematically spending time staying in touch with key people (since hallway conversations were less frequent) and ensuring that her office's contributions were so compelling they had to be included. Her noble, necessary purpose trumped even the apparently implacable demands of Washington power politics.

As Myers's story demonstrates, a corollary to the "more than money" aspect of noble purpose is *external* recognition that an organization is tackling something worth fighting for. In the long run, more than money or profits, widespread external recognition based on noble purpose and hard-fought compromise fuels an organization in very fundamental ways. Recognition motivates employees, makes tensions and struggles worthwhile, and drives people to achieve the best possible outcomes.

CASE STUDY: *"The Campaign for Real Beauty": Dove Flies High*

- **The Intangibility Test:** Self-esteem is hard to quantify, but everyone knows it counts.
- **The Energizing Test:** Employees around the globe worked endless hours to help their wives, sisters, mothers, aunts, and daughters.
- **The Respect Test:** How much does a company benefit when Oprah says they're working to create a better world?

It may seem ironic to turn to the beauty industry to look for a right fight—especially when the issue is purpose. How can a business that depends on superficial, unrealistic, often demoralizing, and even exploitative depictions of women to turn a profit provide important lessons about noble purpose, personal growth, or productive tension? But it is these apparently contradictory circumstances that make this case example so interesting. For several years, Unilever's Dove brand defied the beauty-business stereotype in a fascinating fight that raised issues much larger than selling soap.

In 2001, under the leadership of Silvia Lagnado and later Fernando Acosta, the Dove global brand team decided to throw conventional wisdom to the winds and launch the "Campaign for Real Beauty." The campaign grew out of the convergence of three imperfectly aligned priorities—need to generate sales growth, pressure to redefine the Dove brand for a new generation of consumers, and a heartfelt desire to build the self-esteem of young women around the globe. After much internal debate between the global brand team and the advertising agency, Dove aired a series of unexpected and award-winning television and print ads.

The now-famous series of ads featured ordinary women of all sizes, races, and shapes instead of glamorous models. The campaign started a small revolution, hitting a real nerve with women fed up with the pressures of trying to look like airbrushed, Photoshopped beauty icons, and placed Dove squarely at odds with influential editors and columnists within the beauty industry. The ads eventually developed a real no-holds-barred edge, challenging women to "talk to their daughters before the beauty industry has a chance to do so."

The campaign, focused on improving the self-esteem of ordinary-looking women everywhere, raised lots of eyebrows within Unilever. The company was in the middle of a painful turnaround and wanted its biggest brands focused on sales growth, not something as ephemeral as redefining "real beauty." But initially, the message worked brilliantly. "Dove Evolution," an ad created for $200,000 as part of a public service effort in Canada, went viral on YouTube and made its way to *The Oprah Winfrey Show* within a week, generating over $150 million in free PR for the brand.

Dove sales peaked, but a battle royal was brewing. Internally, the campaign caused significant dissension. Unilever markets many brands in the beauty space—among them Axe, Lifebuoy, Lux, Pond's, Close up, Sunsilk, and Vaseline—and none of them was aligned with the Dove message of real beauty. Several of these brands, in fact, were actively courting fashion-conscious consumers, looking to the opinions and endorsements of the very editors and journalists the Dove campaign had begun to alienate. Critics within the company argued that it was unwise to upset channels and powerful influencers, and that Dove's approach defied best-practice advice to maximize synergy among the various arrows in the Unilever quiver.

Externally, competitors were quick to react. It was only a matter of time before detractors targeted the inconsistent messages within Unilever's brand portfolio. Ads appeared on YouTube nailing Axe deodorant's promise of "winning in the dating game" by parodying the Dove Evolution tagline and asking parents to talk to their children before Unilever did. Procter & Gamble ran a gritty, graphic series of ads targeting the flagship and cash cow of the Dove brand, the beauty bar, as dirty and unhygienic. P&G ads sold body wash by showing a hapless model reacting to pubic hair on her bar soap.

In the face of these internal and external challenges, the Dove team missed its step. Just as the brand's relatively easy expansion into emerging growth markets was complete, P&G's body wash products began to win share points over bar soap in mature markets. The Dove team failed to reexamine what their noble purpose meant in this new environment and how customers connected with it. Body wash is ten times worse for the environment than bar soap, but the team held on to the old fight around real beauty.

Eventually, the internal Dove teams were broken up and redistributed along category rather than brand lines. Dove's brief, stirring defense of "real beauty" faded into the background, and beauty products companies went back to selling as much soap as possible—no doubt with a sigh of relief in many quarters.

But the "Campaign for Real Beauty" was a right fight. It generated some of the most innovative and creative advertising seen in decades. It radically accelerated the brand's penetration around the globe. The internal debate the campaign created between brands was healthy for Unilever as well, requiring the company to refine and refocus its core mission. This was not petty internal infighting about perks, reporting structures, and parking spaces. This was a struggle about something far more important to employees, to consumers— and to women everywhere.

At the campaign's heart was a galvanizing, energizing noble purpose. The marketing team turned the beauty world upside down and Dove's loyal customer base rallied around it. The focus was outside the organization, intangible but still powerful—questioning the very meaning of the brand's mission, searching for a new way to sell products in the future, making customers feel better about themselves.

Unfortunately, even truly right fights don't guarantee permanent success in a rapidly changing environment. Fighting the right fight is at its core a *discipline*, not an event. Even in pursuit of a noble purpose, the future of any enterprise remains a moving target. You have to stay focused there to ultimately triumph.

CASE STUDY: *Hitting a High Note: The Symphony Orchestra Hires a New Leader*

- **The Intangibility Test:** More than ticket sales totals, musical creativity was at stake.
- **The Energizing Test:** Guest conductors brought in a broad range of musical possibility.
- **The Respect Test:** Could the orchestra honor a great leader and still grow beyond him?

When the new executive director of the symphony orchestra took on the position, he was well aware of the great reputation of the long-time musical director, and the great pride with which this midsized city embraced its musical and artistic excellence. Indeed, the orchestra and the musical director were virtually synonymous, and both were important cultural icons for the city. The musical director had been in his position more than twenty years, and along with a few dedicated members of the board, had built the orchestra to what it was today. The orchestra had a loyal following of subscribers—and the musical director was widely known throughout the city, not just by classical music subscribers. What the executive director didn't fully realize was that the musical director had created his reputation by means of a very autocratic management style. He certainly wasn't expecting to collaborate on the musical season with the new executive director.

The new executive director was a musician in his own right, having been known as a virtuoso of the French horn before he began his administrative career in the music world.

As the executive director learned the ins and outs of the organization, it became clear to him that the orchestra had a problem with stagnation. The musical director had been a dominant force for twenty-five years, and it was time for some new thinking. One clear sign of trouble was that the musical director had recently feuded with the musicians' union. The brief strike that followed, though resolved, was still poisoning the atmosphere, making innovation even more difficult.

The board of the orchestra was hoping that the new executive director would reinvigorate the musicians, ease the tensions, and move the organization forward. The executive director's research showed him that despite the name recognition of the musical director, ticket subscriptions were declining, and there were other long-term trends that did not bode well. The organization was dysfunctional, the orchestra members frustrated and disengaged, and the problems began at the top with the musical director.

Something had to be done. The executive director first tried a direct and collaborative approach, meeting with the musical director and engaging him in discussion of the issues the data revealed about the status of the organization. He urged the musical director to create a season that would turn around the bad numbers. The musical director made it clear he was not interested in collaboration—on issues of musical vision or anything else.

Seeking alternatives, the executive director spent time getting to know the orchestra members, the staff, and the board. What did they really want? Many members of the board were still committed to the musical director but were also eager for positive change. Was there a way to have both? To find out, the executive director realized he would have to start a right fight—a fight for the life, vitality, and sustainable future of the organization.

In order to break the stranglehold on the orchestra's innovation and energy, the executive director needed to create a compelling change that would translate into possibility for a new future. Knowing it would be counterproductive to undermine the musical director or to question his long contract, the executive director decided to ask the board to give him responsibility for bringing in guest conductors. In this way he could begin to open things up musically, long before they would have normally started inviting guest conductors as part of the search for a new musical director.

Many board members worried about the growing tension between the musical director and the executive director. But in working with him, they realized the executive director was not asking for more responsibility in order to grow his own base of power. They understood his was not a fight for personal advantage, but a fight to unleash the energy of the whole organization. They recognized and respected the executive director's commitment to the orchestra's noble purpose—its ability to grow and develop its music and its mission to contribute to the civic life of the city.

In the end, despite the musical director's objections, the board gave the executive director authority to bring in the guest conductors. With this new responsibility, the executive director breathed new life into the orchestra. Because of his extended network, many guest conductors accepted invitations, even if they didn't know much about the symphony. The executive director was careful to use his new power to create opportunities for learning and growth, not to undermine the existing musical director. He did not focus on succession candidates; rather, he focused on bringing in conductors with a very wide range of styles, approaches, and experience.

Everyone changed as a result of the diversity of musical styles offered by the guest conductors. Musicians, staff, and the audience all got excited about being part of a wider range of music making, and at the same time, came to appreciate the gifts of the current musical director in a whole new way. Orchestra members became more flexible and more engaged. But it was not an easy time. People were excited, but passions flared and disagreements often turned personal. The executive director had to mediate an extremely delicate balancing act between honoring the current musical director and creating the possibility of a new future.

After a few years, there was growing enthusiasm in the orchestra for one particular guest conductor. When the current musical director became aware of the enthusiasm for this conductor, though it was at first very painful for him, he realized it was time for him to leave. After a complex negotiation, he agreed to end his contract early. When the word got out that he was leaving, several other organizations quickly sought him out. This decision freed orchestra members and the executive director to express their great admiration for the man. As they reached for their new future, the symphony had a great final season with their musical director, and was able to send him off to his new position with genuine gratitude. The symphony even asked him to come back and guest conduct at least once a year.

In the years that followed, the symphony orchestra became musically stronger than ever. Subscriptions went up, and the new musical director became a welcome presence in the community. Because the executive director and his team stayed focused on the organization's noble purpose and on its ultimate goals, they were able to navigate potentially treacherous waters and triumph in a right fight for the orchestra's future.

LEARN *to* FIGHT RIGHT FIGHTS RIGHT: *The* RIGHT FIGHT DISCIPLINE PRINCIPLES

SEVEN

Right Fight Principle #4:
Make It Sport, Not War

YOU'VE MADE IT material. You're focused on the future. And you have a strong sense of purpose to energize you. You know it's a right fight. You know the tensions that exist in your organization can be channeled into positive outcomes. But how do you proceed? Are there disciplined rules of engagement that keep right fights from spiraling into wrong ones?

Fortunately, there are. And, like the principles that identify right fights, these rules of engagement can be learned fairly quickly. Applying them effectively takes sensitivity and finesse, but keeping them in mind makes all the difference in the middle of the fight.

SPORT VERSUS WAR

The first Right Fight Discipline Rule is to make it sport, not war. There are profound differences between being in a fight that feels like sport and one that is all-out war.

Of course, no matter how cutthroat the competition, people don't really lose their lives in business struggles. But people in business often cross lines and make the fights they engage in the wrong ones, even when what's at stake is really worth fighting for. When the consequences of losing exceed the benefits of victory, or when a huge firestorm rages over an issue that is in fact very small, a business battle can start to feel like warfare.

Everyone knows there are supposed to be rules of war. But even so, friendly fire, collateral damage, and civilian casualties are all too common. Things may get sorted out in the end—usually by the victor or those with enough power or influence to remain standing—but then again, they may not. And often the loser gets either the short end of the stick or no stick at all.

IS IT SPORT?—CHECK THE RULEBOOK

In sport, however, the situation is different. Sports have rulebooks. Those rulebooks are available to players, coaches, commentators, and spectators alike. The rulebooks are accessible and authoritative, so all the rules are clear before contestants enter the arena. And if one side or one player starts violating the rules or trying to run rampant over the competition, penalties apply or the rule breaker has to forfeit the match. Rules are the very basis of sporting competition. Sportsmanship requires comportment and discipline.

Right fights, like sports, have to have rules. One of the key tasks for leadership in a right fight is to define the parameters so everyone involved understands how to participate and what it takes to win.

When Mukhtar Kent took over the reins of Coca-Cola, the best-known brand in the world, tensions between headquarters in Atlanta and local bottlers were hardened from decades of wrangling. Kent realized that implementing Coke's "manifesto for growth" required very different approaches in different parts of the globe. Kent developed a rulebook that took into account the dynamics of specific markets in the context of what the organization needed to accomplish on a global basis.

Setting different parameters for different geographies within the company, Kent was able to use his rulebook to escalate pressure where appropriate and to dial it down as needed. Developing a meaningful and customized rulebook made it possible for Kent to manage many different right fights, each carefully designed according to the needs of its particular market, without creating chaos, confusion, or conflict for the larger organization.

IS IT SPORT?—WATCH THE REFEREE

The second important difference between sport and war is that in sport there is someone to enforce the rules. It's the same with right fights. The referee's importance is clear in some of the cases we looked at in previous chapters—like Rolf Classon's right fight or President Reagan's tactics with his speechwriters.

Jack Welch's strategy to identify his successor at GE offers an object lesson in how to be an effective right fight referee. Welch laid down clear rules: the three candidates could not do anything overt to sabotage their peers. He also made it clear he would pay attention and enforce the rules. All three candidates would find CEO positions somewhere if they followed the rules, but Welch would torpedo their careers if they did not. It was a masterful way to determine the leadership characteristics of the three men.

The role of the referee is critical to a right fight. It's also one of the hardest things for senior leaders to do well. In most conflicts, leaders have a favorite idea going in or a preference for one side over another. But to get positive results and to ensure the fight stays right, leaders have to set up the rules and referee the competition without regard to their personal preferences.

When A. G. Lafley took over in 2000 as CEO of P&G, the storied consumer products company, the business was hurting. The company wasn't making its numbers, and the stock price reflected the bad news. It was down 50 percent in the previous six months, a loss of more than $50 billion in market value. Lafley tells the story in his book, *The Game-Changer: How You Can Drive Revenue and Profit Growth with Innovation* (Lafley and Charan, Crown Business, 2008).

The new CEO instituted three major changes to the way

P&G was doing business. Lafley redefined the core mission to put the consumer at the center of everything P&G did. Then he refocused the company on innovation to drive sustained organic growth. But he also implemented a new game plan to compel P&G's people to think about innovation in new ways.

Traditionally, P&G was known as a "not invented here" company. Lafley knew better. He set a startling goal: "We will partner 50 percent of our innovations with outsiders." He watched the data and tracked progress toward this goal himself, making sure people knew he was serious about the issue and would hold them accountable for their commitment to it.

Lafley started from the premise that it is possible to run innovation programs in much the same way you run a factory. To explore different approaches to the innovation problem, P&G created "innovation factories" in each business unit and gave each of them discrete funding, resources, and clear processes for engagement.

To make his vision a reality, Lafley committed to stay deeply involved as cheerleader, coach, and referee. He worked hard with his top teams, and he checked in often with his trusted thinking partner and sounding board, Ram Charan. "Are we getting this right? How do we create enough creative tension in the system to drive our pipeline *and* make innovation something everyone wants to work on?"

As referee, Lafley took pains to make sure the process was fair. Expecting people to open up and engage in the kind of give-and-take that promotes new thinking is asking them to take real personal risks. All participants needed to know that if they didn't win a particular battle, they could come back and try again—and win another time. Innovation thrived in P&G's institutionalized centers and processes because the ref's expectations were simple and unambiguous: practice, learn, and try again.

The results? "From fiscal 2001 through 2007," Lafley says, "even against a background of rising energy and commodity costs, we have improved operating margins by more than four percentage points. Profits have more than tripled to $10-plus billion while free cash flow has totaled $50 billion over the same period. Innovation-driven value creation and incremental sales growth from innovation have nearly doubled since 2001. That has helped us average 12 percent earnings per share growth and increase our market cap by $100 billion, making us one of the ten most valuable companies in the United States."

Organizations like P&G have learned that a referee is essential. In a productive right fight, the referee works to surface underlying tensions so that battle lines are clear and everyone is heard. That process is counterintuitive for most organizations. Most companies tend to conceal or smooth over deep divides in the mistaken belief that the appearance of unity is the best way to get business done. It is far more productive, however, when an effective referee uses the energy present in the tensions between opposing viewpoints to move things forward.

IS IT SPORT?—LEVEL THE PLAYING FIELD

The neutrality of the referee and the existence of rules are not quite enough to ensure that a right fight is fought right.

You also have to make sure that you've got a level playing field. Each side has to have a real chance to win. Preemptive strikes using overwhelming force may be an advantage in warfare, but they render a right fight both meaningless and impossible.

Of course it's true that competitions are rarely matched in a way that's perfectly even. Each of the opposing sides has strengths and each has disadvantages. There can be clear front-runners and definite underdogs. But a fight whose outcome is a foregone conclusion is not a right fight, and it is unlikely to generate anything but lackluster effort, humiliation, and resentment.

Over the last few years, the manufacturing leadership team at Shell Oil has been engaged in a turnaround of safety and reliability performance at the energy giant's refineries and chemical sites. Shell's right fight is to implement a "reliability-driven strategy" that holds refinery and site leaders responsible for lowering costs and improving the availability of their equipment *at the same time*—clearly not an easy thing to do.

Conventional wisdom argues that to move to top performance in reliability, you first have to spend money to improve physical plant facilities, a move that necessarily results in less effective control of costs. But given the volatile nature of oil prices in the past several years, conventional wisdom was never going to get Shell's manufacturing group the rapid performance improvement they were seeking.

Working under three different CEOs in a two-year time frame, the leadership team decided to move the tension point from refinery site leaders to frontline managers. Refining is operationally complex, and it's the frontline managers who best understand the infinitely fluctuating trade-offs between operating performance, maintenance, and reliability. The move, though, was controversial. Shell had spent years defining and standardizing operations and maintenance processes in an attempt to maximize reliability and minimize expense around the globe.

But the global processes had their limits. Shell's separate maintenance and operations management groups lacked flexibility and responsiveness in dealing with specific problems at individual refineries. Repair requests from operations had to wait for prioritization by maintenance, resulting in backlogs of weeks or months at times. When maintenance finally showed up to do repairs, operations didn't have affected units off-line and work couldn't be completed. Frustrations were high as operations and maintenance leaders blamed the process and each other for poor performance. In the new two-pronged initiative, senior leaders of the company were attempting to align hundreds of local decisions that individually matter very little, but globally make a huge difference on both fronts.

Initial pilots of the initiative were extremely promising. At one refinery, a group of exemplary frontline managers focused on improving the maintenance and operations interface for certain critical utility systems that take toxic sulfur compounds and sulfuric acid out of steam. In just a few weeks of operation, the pilot program cut maintenance backlogs in half, improved time on tools for operators and maintenance craftsmen, and cut overall maintenance costs by 30 percent. Interestingly, employee satisfaction scores in the unit went from an average of six to an average of nine out of ten. And the team didn't have to throw out the global process structure to make it work.

The site's operations leader, James Rhame, leveled the playing field by forcing maintenance and operations groups to work together to improve results. He set clear expectations and rules, made resources available, and refereed conflict but didn't tell the frontline leaders what to do. He called on the managers' competitive spirit to see if they could beat the rest of the plant's maintenance performance. And he made sure that his best frontline leaders were coaching the pilot team along the way. It was a real right fight fought right.

Rhame's success in leveling the playing field at Shell demonstrates how beneficial it can be to mine disagreements for their underlying energy. At the outset, there wasn't much agreement between the members of the refinery's exemplary managers' team on how to proceed. The managers had very different ideas about how to improve performance, and those ideas were in tension with global corporate maintenance procedures.

It's a common misconception that teamwork is all about agreement. It's not. Effective teams begin with real differences of opinion on most aspects of the task at hand. They need to agree on only one thing, but it's the single most important thing to get right—the goal. As long as unity around the goal is clear, teams can have and *should* have big disagreements about tactics, ways of overcoming obstacles, and other actions along their journey to that goal. That's what makes it not war, but sport.

CASE STUDY: *Microsoft Exterminates Bugs—Patty Stonesifer Takes on Leadership in Tech Support*

- **The Rulebook:** A rewrite of tech-support charge-back policy promised improved performance in tech support and product lines.
- **The Ref:** Bill Gates committed himself to oversee and enforce the rules.
- **The Playing Field:** Could tech support even get into the game with product developers and managers?

By the time Bill Gates asked Patty Stonesifer to fix the Microsoft tech-support organization in the early 1990s, the situation had become a disaster. Customers calling for help might wait on hold for an hour or more, only to get a technician who didn't have a clue what the answer was, or one who dropped the call. Some calls never got answered at all. Even in Microsoft's heyday, Bill knew this was unsustainable, but the price tag to fix the problems looked staggering.

Enter Patty Stonesifer. At first, she applied the obvious fixes: she repaired trunk lines, improved morale, put in call-answering systems, changed schedules, trained techs.

Six months in, though, it was clear to Stonesifer that however much she improved the tech centers, everything she did led to rising costs and rising expectations. Not only was it hard to see how she could achieve the goal for tech support performance, it was hard even to know what the goal was. Given the trend data, whatever she tried would eventually cost too much.

The root of the problem was that the products were too "buggy" when they were released. The way Microsoft ran things, each individual product was charged back at cost for its share of tech-support activity. Product managers preferred to pay the tech-support charge backs because that was cheaper than fixing the bugs when the trade-offs were to sacrifice new functionality or to delay release dates. Attempts to persuade the product engineers of the "moral rightness" of fixing known bugs fell on deaf ears. Call-center staff were lower than second-class citizens. How could Stonesifer level the playing field so tech support could succeed?

Stonesifer devised a plan that required Gates, herself, and a small group of product-development executives to decide each year which kinds of bugs should be addressed in each new release. Working this list took time and judgment; bugs that were acceptable in early stages of product development became less so as the product matured. Some bugs were more annoying to customers than others. Some created big problems on large networks.

Based on the list, Microsoft made charge backs for certain types of bugs increasingly expensive. Product groups did not have to fix bugs in any given release if those fixes weren't at the top of the priority lists, but over time, it would become increasingly expensive not to fix them. This put the trade-off back in the business hands of the product leadership and forced real collaboration with the tech center.

Stonesifer had created new rules of play, with Gates refereeing the game. And it worked. The day after launch, the call center was filled with product engineers trying to figure out how to eliminate bugs. To try to keep bugs off the "expensive list," product developers invested significant time with tech-support staff in how things really worked. The value of call-center knowledge skyrocketed.

From a traditional perspective, not being charged back at cost wasn't fair, but at the company level, it was a brilliant way to greatly increase quality and keep tech costs from spiraling out of control. It was sport rather than war, and it solved the problem. It also got tech support and the product teams working together on fixes rather than ignoring each other.

By creating a system that awarded product groups for performance (and penalized them for being slow to produce solutions), Stonesifer provoked a right fight that vastly improved Microsoft's consumer tech support. The product groups and tech groups understood the rules and knew just who was monitoring them, and everyone came to see the intervention as effective. Stonesifer relied on sportsmanship rather than warfare, and she achieved winning results.

Patty Stonesifer's right fight kept the larger good of the whole organization in focus and allowed both the tech and the product sides to reap the rewards of victory. When the goal is shared and victory benefits even the losing side, extremely contentious and difficult fights can end in a way that satisfies everyone.

CASE STUDY: *Revitalizing IT—Johnson & Johnson's IT Transformation Creates Value for All*

- **The Rulebook:** J&J wrote new rules for IT structure and processes.
- **The Referee:** New global CIO LaVerne Council led the way, personally taking on the role of "head coach."
- **The Playing Field:** Can a real, enduring partnership be built between a company and its major vendors? Is it worth fighting for?

LaVerne Council took on an enormous challenge when she became the first global chief information officer and corporate vice president of Johnson and Johnson in 2006. Founded in 1886, Johnson & Johnson began selling the world's first sterile surgical dressings, and innovation in the health care field has remained central to its mission.

Johnson & Johnson, through its 250 operating companies, is a broad-based manufacturer of health care products and services, for the consumer, pharmaceutical, and medical devices and diagnostics markets. This position has been achieved by concentrating on human health, following the ethical principles embodied in the Johnson & Johnson Credo, and managing the business for the long term.

The Credo, which can be found on the company's Web site in thirty-two languages, outlines Johnson & Johnson's responsibilities to customers, employees, local communities, and stockholders. It focuses on respect for individual dignity, managing ethically, and making a fair profit.

In 2006, when Council became Global CIO, the IT organization mirrored the company's decentralized structure across the multiple regions and business sectors. Recognizing that change was needed, Johnson & Johnson leadership hired Council with high expectations. They expected her to realign IT to realize economies of scale that were not part of the organization's operating model. They wanted decisive action but not at the price of violating the company's long-held values or undermining the individual operating companies. In short, she had to abide by the Credo but somehow achieve the expected results.

In a decentralized culture, centralizing authority means making the tough calls and, in some cases, relieving people of responsibilities they would prefer to keep. Many people inside the company were resistant to change and some doubted Council could succeed.

For years, Johnson & Johnson's companies had seen IT as an ever-increasing cost to their operations, not as a source of business value. Council's initial challenge was to persuade the operating companies to cost share with her office on new initiatives because her own budget was minimal.

To build support, she spent her first hundred days on the road talking to all the business heads and anyone else who would listen, persuading them that it was time to start reaping economies of scale. She was delighted to discover that many of the business units were eager to sign up. They wanted better IT systems and were enthusiastic to cooperate with someone who was promising a leap forward in capability at lower cost.

Council rewrote the rulebook through a great deal of discussion and consensus building. The executive committee supported her plan to establish direct reporting relationships with the CIOs of the major product divisions as well as the heads of the other major IT functional areas. She focused her efforts on developing the existing leadership group into a team capable of working together—something they hadn't been asked to do before. Together, they undertook a major program to design and implement an IT strategy built around three pillars—Improve, Transform, and Innovate—with the goal of transforming IT into a recognized driver of business value.

Armed with a focused strategy built through consensus, Council began to establish herself as a fair, yet tough head coach for the IT function and referee between IT and multiple stakeholders. Early on, she and the leadership team worked to centralize and modernize vendor relationships as a major source of value to the company. Historically, the IT leaders in the various businesses had their own contracts with vendors—for everything from computers and phone systems, to networks, systems programming, and IT support. The company did not have a single IT master service agreement; everything was purchased on an a la carte basis. Vendors sold IT services via small, expensive, individually negotiated contracts with various operating companies.

Council established a new group within IT called IT Global Services and mandated that all contracts with vendors for application design, development, and support go through this group. In addition, the IT Strategic Sourcing group would be the point of contact for all other vendors of hardware, software, and other IT components. So any vendor that wanted to partner with Johnson & Johnson had to commit to work through these groups and live up to the values and practices stated in the Credo. Vendors also had to make significant changes in the way they did business with Johnson & Johnson by focusing on a very different kind of value proposition, cost structure, and commitment of resources to the company.

The IT Global Services and Strategic Sourcing groups asked vendors to respond to formal Requests For Proposals (RFPs) for enterprise-wide service agreements. Under Council's leadership, the bidding process became highly competitive but on a level playing field. Council directed the teams to consider all enterprise bids equally with no advantage for vendors who had previous contracts with Johnson & Johnson operating companies in an attempt to create fair and open competition. Some of the major vendors didn't believe in her game plan so they played the old way. They lost.

Early on, Council set the tone by letting the vendors know her expectations on how the bid process and contract negotiations would be handled. One major vendor won the global enterprise contract for a set of services. Part of the deal was that the vendor would do all business at Johnson & Johnson through IT Global Services, at the enterprise price—no more selling directly to operating companies.

Sometimes, old habits are hard to break and the inevitable happened. A business unit of the vendor that won the enter-

prise contract, a very large company in its own right, con-
tracted for work directly with a Johnson & Johnson operating
company and at a different price. This action violated the
terms of the enterprise deal.

When the deal became known, the vendor sent the president of its North American business to Council with an expla-
nation, an apology, and a promise that it would not happen
again. The spotlight was now on Council—how would she
handle this? Many people expected her to accept the apology
and move forward in the spirit of partnership. After all, it was
a mistake.

"If you make nice when they do something wrong the
first time," Council said, "it's like a wife who doesn't protest
when her husband misbehaves the first time. That's when you
have to come down clear and tough! This is precisely the time
to create a right fight—to fight for building a relationship you
can count on to deliver, not one where nice people apologize
while value and trust are subtly undermined. Great partnerships are worth fighting for—they don't just happen because
everyone is nice and tries hard."

Council said to the vendor, "We play by the rules here.
I'm not interested in your excuses; what I want to know is
what you're going to do make this right. You can start by
taking this seriously enough to send your CEO. And when
you do, please have him come with a set of options for what
we will do for each other that makes this right, not another
apology."

Council asked for concessions—a better enterprise price, a
new vendor relationship manager, and cash to invest in build-

ing better processes between the vendor and Johnson & Johnson. Her demands were focused on deepening the relationship until it really developed into a partnership—because that's where the real value is found. Both sides needed to know the rules were real and that failure had real consequences.

The vendor balked at first but that changed very quickly once its CEO realized how serious Council was about working with them. They worked out a new deal that was equitable to both sides. Johnson & Johnson got a better price, but not as much as Council would have liked. A new vendor relationship manager took over to work with the right person in IT Global Services. The vendor received another larger assignment that made it more economical to invest in start-up costs and help develop the partnership.

Council succeeded in making sure the deal fit the Credo and that it benefited both sides. Everyone involved now understood that Council fought fairly but also wanted to win—with a focus on value, transparency, and strict business ethics.

The implications of this situation went far beyond the deal with this vendor. Johnson & Johnson employees across the globe now understood that Council would fight for what was right while ensuring firm but fair competition . . . to her, it was sport, not war.

Two years later, this right fight is still going on. IT has delivered extraordinary value and made great strides in moving from the Improve stage of the IT strategy to Transform and Innovate. Yet, there is still much work to do to deliver on the promise of innovation that drives the efficacy and efficiency of health care for Johnson & Johnson and for people across the globe. Under Council's leadership, Johnson & Johnson IT is prepared to go the distance.

The redirection of Johnson & Johnson IT had the potential to undermine and enervate the company if the fights had turned into an all-out battle about turf, authority, and budgets. Sadly, this is too often the case between IT and business units, and between IT and vendors. Council's commitment to structure right fights like a sport—developing a winning game plan with clear rules, a code of conduct, and a level playing field—allowed Johnson & Johnson IT, operating companies, and vendors to transform relationships into partnerships in a positive and highly productive way.

In considering the importance of making a right fight seem like sport and not war, you start to understand why traditional efforts at team building often seem like a waste of time. Rafting together can help a little around the edges, because building personal trust among team members does make the job of working out compromise agreements a little easier. The problem is that issues with expertise, trust, and structural tension still remain unresolved after the team has shot through the rapids on the company retreat and headed back to the office to get things done.

Structuring disagreements as right fights works to capture the energy inherent in tension, just as a game between rival sports teams invigorates and engages its participants. In right fights, just as in sports, everyone wins at least occasionally. The participants believe the contest is fair, and they accept the outcome—if not happily, at least gracefully enough to stay in the league and keep competing.

Making a right fight sport, not war, means having a solid game plan and playing by the rules. It means the leader sets expectations, energizes the team to win, and assures a well-fought contest. And all involved have to believe that they will live to fight another day. In a right fight, victory is not permanent and defeat is never total. The losing side should always leave with something—even if it's just an invitation to come back later for a rematch.

EIGHT

Right Fight Principle #5: Structure Formally but Work Informally

WE'VE JUST LOOKED at how important it is for right fights to have rules, referees, and reasonably matched opposing sides. Making it sport, not war, means conducting your fight in a clean, functional environment where boundary lines are marked and the stakes are declared up front. This structural context is important because without it, fights don't stay right. They risk devolving into messy, protracted civil wars that bog down everyone and prevent organizations from moving forward.

There is a particular structural context in which right fights are most productive for all involved, and that context is described in our second Right Fight Discipline Principle. You need to structure right fights through the "formal organization," but work out the tensions created by those fights through the "informal organization."

STRUCTURE FORMALLY—EXPLOIT THE GAPS

Formal organizational structure is easy for most people to identify. When you ask someone to describe the company he is part of, he will most likely describe aspects of its *formal* organization—org charts, who reports to whom, how governance and decision making are supposed to work. Especially in large organizations, there is plenty of formal structure to identify because there are many subsets of the overall alignment system: which group is responsible for which priorities, who has the P&L, what is a cost center, which groups are shared service providers, and so on.

In her book *The Third Opinion*, Saj-nicole looked at how these alignment subsets work to establish what she calls *structural trust* and its opposite, *structural tension*, within organizations. High structural trust exists when interests are aligned, because people expect certain behaviors and attitudes from others based simply on their positions, functions, or roles.

A medium level of structural trust is necessary for an organization to function effectively; if it gets too low, if everywhere you look you find misaligned goals and objectives, it becomes impossible to function. But the truth is there are lots of potential gaps in the system, lots of places where objectives, roles, and rewards are at least partially misaligned. Salespeople will tend to set forecasts low so they can beat their quotas. Finance folks like to question expenses and push on costs. R&D people fixate on the latest technology, science, or innovation. Marketing execs focus on brand, image, and reputation. These are structural tensions.

In fact, most CEOs raise and lower structural tensions at different times, seeking results. At all levels, we have found skillful leaders who purposefully exploit and often even create areas of imperfect alignment. They rely on team members to develop clear but conflicting advocacy positions around the misalignment, based on their differing roles, biases, and perspectives. Tensions will be high because the team members have different priorities, but a right fight between the various positions offers tremendous opportunity for discovery and development.

The Shell example we saw in the previous chapter is a prime example of the benefits you can achieve by exploiting gaps in structural trust. At Shell, there was a significant gap between the maintenance group, which focused heavily on repair costs and craftsmen productivity, and the operations side, which prioritized uptime and product margins.

Since the wide gap between maintenance and operations was impacting overall plant performance, the company first tried to bridge it by means of a new global maintenance scheduling process. But instead of solving the problem, the fix actually exacerbated it. Maintenance focused even more intensively on critical repairs, scheduling less important procedures in the distant future. Operations responded by labeling every repair a critical priority but continued to keep equipment online when maintenance teams showed up to do scheduled work.

Shell's James Rhame recognized the productive potential

within the structural impasse. By creating a single team of exemplary frontline managers, he pulled together a group that accurately reflected all the underlying roles and biases and could hammer out compromises in real-time, one-on-one interactions. The global process stayed in place and competing priorities continued to drive the groups, but the exemplary team worked within the gap toward end results that did in fact both lower costs and improve reliability—dramatically.

WORK INFORMALLY—RELY ON RELATIONSHIPS

In his right fight at Shell, Rhame structured formally, expecting the managers on the exemplary team to represent their groups' interests and to respect the global process. But he also structured the team so that people, working together, could trump the formal structure and process when necessary in order to get things done.

To put it another way, Rhame called on the power of the *informal* organization to accomplish what the formal organizational structure at Shell had not. Anyone with real experience in real organizations knows that this is often the way work actually gets done—not along the org chart pathways but across them.

The tissues of relationship that cross formal boundary lines, the loose networks that people in groups tend to form with others who have similar interests, experiences, or preferences, are the essence of the informal organization. Informal organizations operate all the time in an almost infinite number of ways and affect an equally large number of interactions—who talks to whom, who has specific expertise, who motivates action, who is a safe confidant, who internally brokers access, relationships, or information.

We all recognize relationships in the informal organization when we see them: the CIO who gets music advice from the VP in marketing who's up on the latest tunes. The two managers, one from accounting, the other from sales, who share a passion for motorcycles. The employees from different divisions who meet most days for lunch to share war stories about their kids who are enrolled in the same school.

Ties in the informal organization are often social, but there are informal professional bonds as well: the R&D scientist whom everyone turns to for the latest on nanotechnology because she's the most knowledgeable expert by miles. The director in accounting who has an uncanny sense for knowing which way the market is heading. The salesperson who just understands the youth market better than anyone else.

The bad news about these informal networks is that they are complex and infinitely nuanced. Because they're the byproducts of hundreds of thousands of interconnected personal relationships, it requires specialized skill to map them precisely and describe them definitively, especially in a large organization. That process, though often extraordinarily productive, requires time and particular resources that may not be readily available in the middle of a conflict.

The good news is that it's actually fairly simple to understand how the informal organization works in general and how to manage it explicitly to improve overall performance. Building bonds in the informal organization is all about increasing the levels of *personal* trust that exist between people.

Relationships Require Trust

Personal trust is something everyone understands. We all know relationships matter. When people know and respect one another, they ask more of each other and are willing to think and act outside the box on each other's behalf. Personal trust grows over time when people share critical tasks and develop an understanding of what makes their colleagues tick. When you've worked late with teammates on a tight deadline, or responded with them to an emergency on a shop floor, you begin to know, and trust, what they are made of.

Various team-building enterprises promise to generate trust relationships between people who haven't had the time, energy, or opportunity to build them organically by working together. Sometimes these programs achieve dramatic results. Far too often, though, the wilderness weekend or the annual retreat fails to have the desired positive impact on a company's people or culture.

The problem is that issues of personal trust have to be resolved within the right context. If people don't trust their colleagues and co-workers to align interests, fulfill commitments, and support projects at work, off-site team building is likely to make people feel better about each other, but not give them the tools to resolve the issues that keep them at cross purposes. If you want to increase the effectiveness and productivity of the informal organization that operates in your workplace, you have to build personal trust relationships *in that work-place*. It's as simple as that.

A few years ago, we worked with the newly appointed CFO of a high-flying Silicon Valley software company. Although the company was doing extremely well, tensions were high. Skyrocketing growth had outpaced the revenue recognition systems and the team was struggling to make the transition from start-up mode to more scalable and predictable business and accounting processes. Two senior finance executives had been brought in from outside the company, one to work on business processes and the other to reengineer accounting. Each new leader hired several people he personally trusted from previous jobs and set out to whip things into shape.

Then the situation escalated from skirmishes to a major siege. Because of irregularities in awarding executive stock options, the company was forced to restate its financial reports. The executives actually responsible for the irregularities had been dismissed, but battle lines developed between the new professional management team and members of the original group who felt pressured to justify past practices.

Tension levels, already high, escalated further. The new team needed to work closely with the old team to create efficient processes and systems that accurately reflected the way the business worked. But the old team was working extremely long hours and on weekends on the restatement and quickly came to resent requests for time not directly related to it. Tempers flared daily as the restatement process dragged on for months and eventually progress came to a halt. An informal poll revealed that a majority of the finance organization was actively looking for a new job.

Over a year into it, the CFO recognized that the restatement had become a classic wrong fight. He personally reached out to build relationships with employees two and three levels down in his organization and developed a firsthand understanding of how people felt in the two camps. Realizing that the entire finance group had never really had the chance to work together, he temporarily suspended all work on the new systems and assigned the new team to help out with the restatement as much as they could.

The extra capacity made a huge difference in the morale of the old team. More important, it gave both groups the chance to roll up their sleeves, do real work together, and see what the other side was really like. The restatement was completed, and 90 percent of both groups stayed with the firm. When the CFO turned his attention back to building new processes and systems for the future, the new team's trial by fire in the old systems proved invaluable. They understood how the systems needed to work and they knew which of the experienced employees they could turn to with specific questions.

In this case, a wrong fight to assign blame for past mistakes turned into a right fight for the future once the CFO stepped outside the formal structures he'd established and worked on nurturing healthy trust relationships in his company's informal organization. Right fights make tension productive, but productive tension requires high levels of personal trust within the team. Trust that colleagues in the opposition will do what they promise and that teammates on your side won't let you down when it counts is what keeps a right fight from degenerating into an unproductive conflict of personalities.

WORK INFORMALLY—INSIST ON IDEAS

Both James Rhame at Shell and the Silicon Valley CFO leveraged the power of informal trust-based networks to solve problems that had hardened into unrelenting silos at the level of the formal organizations. Silos are, to some extent, an unavoidable hazard of organizational life, since structural trust dictates that people will necessarily adopt at least some of the functional biases attached to their professional roles. But as the Shell and Silicon Valley examples show, leaders can breach silos by tapping the resource of personal trust between colleagues.

As we saw in Chapter 5, right fights only happen where there is real uncertainty about the best answer, so a right fight's very existence indicates that the path ahead isn't crystal clear. To position a fight productively, you need accurate information about what's going on at ground level and creative ideas about how to move forward. These ideas are powerful, necessary, sometimes divergent, and often hard to get.

Warren Bennis, Daniel Goleman, and James O'Toole define the problem in their book, *Transparency* (Jossey-Bass, 2008):

> There may have been a time when an imperial leader
> could know everything an organization needed to know
> to be successful. But if such a time ever existed, it is long

gone. Today, the information an organization needs may be located anywhere, including outside. And the leader who has a narrow view of proper channels for information often pays a high price for its orderly but insufficient flow.

A universal problem is that when staff speak to their leader, the very nature of the message tends to change. The message is likely to be spun, softened, and colored in ways calculated to make it more acceptable to the person in power. In order to continue to receive reliable information, those in power must be aware that whatever they hear from their direct reports has probably been heavily edited, if only to make the message more palatable and to make the messenger appear more valuable. And so wise leaders find ways to get information raw.

This is where the power of your networks in the informal organization is essential. Staying within the constructs of the formal organization will leave you hopelessly out of touch. Managers who rely only on the hierarchy for information constantly underestimate the levels of stress in their direct reports and overestimate the willingness of subordinates to take on more work and tension. When structural constraints and formal hierarchy prevent you from accessing the information you need, the informal organization offers an effective solution.

Saj-nicole's book *The Third Opinion* emphasizes how important it is for leaders to access and deploy relationships based on *expertise* trust as they go about the business of leading. Expertise trust is trust that comes from someone's competence and knowledge in a particular subject matter or process. It's the kind of trust that allows you to fly on a jet or have orthopedic surgery—you trust the expertise of the pilot or the surgeon even though you know virtually nothing about them other than that they are trained and licensed to do their highly specialized jobs.

Wise leaders take advantage of expert advice. They use the relational resources of the informal organization to locate experts and ideas at lower organizational levels and they seek outside sources. Especially for leaders at the topmost levels of hierarchy, what Saj-nicole refers to as "third opinions" from trusted outside experts can yield valuable insights and fresh alternatives not available in the leaders' own thinking or in the second opinions they hear from others inside the organization.

In Chapter 5, we also looked at Rolf Classon's classic right fight for the future. His story demonstrates the crucial importance of accessing expertise-based relationships and encouraging alternative ideas in working through the tensions of a right fight.

The acquisition that was pending when Classon took over as CEO was almost a done deal. Resistance to it within the organization was buried several layers below the chairman's office, but Classon paid attention to what he sensed within the informal organization. He made it possible for resistance to safely bubble up through the hierarchy and be heard.

Classon listened objectively to the various opinions within the company, and he solicited third opinions from unbiased outside experts. In the end, Classon's initial intuition proved accurate. The resistance he first heard about through informal channels held the seeds of issues that, when fully explored, enabled the new leadership to reevaluate the deal. It still seemed to make economic sense, but came up lacking in terms of strategic focus on their consumer portfolio. They passed on the deal, and were handsomely rewarded when a much more strategically attractive deal was completed within the following eighteen months.

Like Classon, great leaders learn how to work out tensions and conflicts through the informal networks that make the formal organization hum. They acknowledge their need for access to unfiltered information and recognize the creative potential in opportunities for unfettered thinking. They leverage their personal and expertise-based relationships in the informal organization to gather information, to gauge employee morale and mood, to allow things to bubble up from the best and the brightest, to test hunches, and to champion ideas.

Beyond that, they set up systems that encourage *everyone* to participate in informal knowledge sharing, creating an open culture radically unlike the "mushroom" environment of far too many companies—where the lower an employee is on the org chart, the more likely he is to be kept in the dark.

CASE STUDY: *Unilever Matrix Reloaded—Patrick Cescau Restructures to Revitalize*

- **The Gap:** Global authority structures were being overruled by country-specific fiefdoms.

- **The Relationships:** Vindi Banga leveraged his personal network to support new global systems and goals.
- **The Ideas**: Was the knowledge base in Banga's network wide and deep enough to support a global organization in turmoil?

Patrick Cescau's first move in 2005 as CEO of the venerable Anglo-Dutch consumer packaged-goods company Unilever was to turn the organization on its head. Unilever had traditionally operated as two holding companies—a foods business and a home and personal care products business. There were two chairmen and duplicate brand organizations all over the world. The countries were king as they managed the real P&Ls and even did most of the brand development to suit local market tastes. This system was not even remotely efficient, since it meant, for example, that there were forty-six varieties of Unilever vanilla ice cream in Western Europe alone.

Cescau reorganized the company, tilting the global matrix in favor of global brands and categories. The goal was clear: bigger, bolder innovations from the center with countries focused on brand building and delivering the plan. The new operating framework was of course controversial and it created huge tensions throughout the 40,000-person organization.

At first, no one was even sure who was calling the shots. To manage the new matrix, leaders were assigned to multiple global teams, which meant they spent their time circling the world attending meetings. Then the company found its footing, and began to grow again, due in large part to the emergence of leaders like Vindi Banga.

Banga had run Hindustan Lever (HLL) for several years. HLL was in itself a huge, complex organization—at that time the largest company in India. Legally a joint venture between Indian shareholders and Unilever shareholders, HLL operated in a rapidly growing economy with limited infrastructure, and its operations were anything but simple.

It was not surprising that Cescau tapped several of HLL's up-and-coming executives for global leadership roles. At Cescau's request, Banga moved to London and took over the global home and personal care (HPC) category team. The team Banga put together for HPC included some of the company's brightest marketers, and it quickly pulled off an impressive string of successful brand repositionings—including the "campaign for real beauty" at Dove.

With many of the HPC brands on a clear path to global growth, Cescau moved Banga over to the more challenging global foods category team. Conventional wisdom said that although there were underlying global trends in demand for laundry detergents, soap, and deodorants that created scale for innovations, food was essentially a local business. But conventional wisdom was wrong.

Banga brought many of the successful category leaders over from HPC into the foods business and began achieving similar successes with his relatively young group of leaders. The introduction of new vitality platforms like cholesterol-lowering margarines and vitamin-rich mini drinks began to revitalize the once low-growth foods business.

How could one individual make such a difference? The answer was Banga's personal network. Having run a major country division for the company, his relationships within the chaotic new world of the global categories were deep. And since the country division he had run was one of the largest and most complex in the world, he had personal experience of what would and would not work in the country organizations.

Banga also leveraged the power of relationships. He encouraged his team to use persuasion and influence rather than exerting crude authority. Those who had known him at HLL, where hierarchy and authority reigned supreme and consensus building was rare, were surprised by the change in style. But Banga knew that his new role required the judicious use of tension in order to get things done. Although the new global categories had formal authority to dictate to the countries, Banga realized it would prove much more effective in the long run to woo them over to the new brand strategies by showing them by example what was possible if they cooperated.

Within his own team he became the decider of last resort, allowing his category leaders the first try at wrestling with resource allocations and prioritization before he stepped in and made a decision for them. At one point it became apparent during a global foods team meeting that the recently approved marketing budget needed to be cut by €20 million. The reduction was relatively small in the overall scheme of things, but the category leaders were understandably hesitant to raise their hands to lower their expense allocations. Banga announced to the group that he would think about it over dinner and announce his cuts to the team the next morning, knowing full well that the category and brand leaders would resolve the issue among themselves over drinks that evening rather than have the decision made for them.

Banga's skill at managing complex relationships came from knowing not only how his team worked together but also what motivated his people individually. When he brought Silvia Lagnado over from HPC to revitalize the savory soups and bouillons business, he asked her to turn the product on its head. Lagnado eliminated most of the salt and glutamates and repositioned the products as a healthy meal alternative for busy moms around the world—a similar tack to the one she took at Dove.

Banga was not an easy boss to work for. He rarely pushed back when Cescau needed to trim category budgets or deferred to country priorities. But in challenging his people and offering them the full value of his own personal network, he created a generation of up and coming category leaders. Some of these leaders, like Alan Jope in spreads and dressings and Peter ter Kulve in ice creams, replicated Banga's model and became global zealots for their own brand categories, creating their own deep relationships with the countries they relied upon so heavily for their success.

Because they knew how to manage tensions through relationships and understood the complexities of the informal network at Unilever, Banga and his team were able to spend their time on right fights around product innovation and brand identity, avoiding the unproductive turf battles so common in other large matrix organizations. It was really no surprise when, before his own retirement, Cescau completed his reorganization, eliminated the HPC and foods divisions entirely, and gave all Unilever's global category organizations to Banga to run.

It's also no surprise that international corporations face all kinds of right-fight-worthy challenges. Structural gaps abound in large, cross-cultural enterprises, and people whose relationship and knowledge networks are extensive enough to bridge the divides are widely sought after for leadership roles. But the challenge of doing *business* across national borders pales in many ways when you compare it to the challenge of doing *good*. The ability to leverage relationships and knowledge productively within structural, organizational, and even governmental gaps is what makes The Acumen Fund successful.

CASE STUDY: *Leveraging Acumen: Making Business into Charity*

- **The Gap:** You name it, Acumen's experienced it— compassion and economic rigor, chaos and systematic rebuilding, despair and uplifting hope.
- **The Relationships:** Acumen portfolio managers hammer out complex negotiations that can mean life or death for affected populations.
- **The Ideas:** How do you find scalable and sustainable solutions to the problems of poverty, disease, and social dislocation?

Most charities trying to improve the lot of humanity—like Save the Children, the World Wildlife Fund, or UNICEF—focus on either a particular problem or a particular country or locale—for example, efforts to help the victims of Hurricane Katrina in the United States or the tsunami in Indonesia. The Acumen Fund aims more broadly to find ways in which markets can complement traditional approaches, using highly innovative and cost-effective ways to better the human condition.

Acumen's mission is to answer the question of scale—how to create programs that can be implemented on a large scale and that enable economically sustainable, lasting improvements in quality of life for the world's poor. The fund invests in a variety of institutions and business models to figure out what will most effectively reach the "base of the pyramid"—the billions of poor worldwide who live on less than four dollars a day and lack access to clean water, reliable health services, permanent housing options, and basic economic choices.

As Jacqueline Novogratz, CEO of the Acumen Fund, sees it, the underlying issue is how to ensure efficiency and at the same time produce broad, meaningful, enduring results through enterprises that make business sense and create societal good. She says, "In this tension lies the hope for real change in our world. Ignore one side of the tension, and you end up helping people in a way that is ultimately unsustainable. Ignore the other side of the tension, and you end up focusing only a shareholder-driven market approach, and cut out a large percentage of the world's population. Only in the tension of *viable economics* and *societal good* are we able to find solutions that enable sustainable progress in developing societies that currently have high levels of injustice for the true poor. You don't survive unless you are very flexible. It's at every level of the way you operate."

Acumen invests in ideas in very concrete ways. For example, in both urban and rural areas of India, low-income households generally lack access to affordable, safe water. Families, especially women and girls, spend long hours collecting water from local water sources and end up with water that is not safe for consumption. An Acumen initiative, Water Health International, developed a model incorporating a cost-effective technology designed for the poor and an effective approach to social marketing and distribution. The business model is unique, combining social marketing expertise, a deep knowledge of local markets, commercial financing skills, and world-class technology for purifying bacterial contamination in collected surface water. The water systems have already given one million people in India alone daily access to safe, affordable water.

Another Acumen company has figured out how to use LED technology to create a light source that is inexpensive, safe, and versatile regarding the power supply—this pioneering technology works through standard power sources, generators, or solar cells. Since more than 1.5 billion people in the world live without electricity, relying on kerosene and candles, the new technology knowledge being leveraged here promises to prevent thousands of crippling injuries and deaths every year due to dangerous lighting, and keep hundreds of thousands of pounds of particulate pollution and greenhouse gases out of the atmosphere.

Acumen efforts are also fighting malaria, a disease that

causes almost 2 million deaths a year. Current treatments have lost their efficacy, and drug-resistant strains are spreading worldwide. By scaling up production of *Artemisia annua,* a plant that produces a key ingredient in a more effective anti-malarial treatment, an Acumen-supported company is providing local jobs in Kenya, Tanzania, and Uganda and a critical supply of affordable malaria treatment worldwide. Selling the raw material to pharmaceutical companies such as Novartis, farmers can earn up to four times the income they would receive for other subsistence crops.

Acumen has no lack of structural gaps to exploit for potentially productive right fights. The gaps that Acumen works within permeate all aspects of its organizational identity. Some gaps are external, governmental lapses or social divisions that complicate Acumen's ability to implement programs. As Novogratz explains, "We were in Pakistan and went to talk to farmers in rural areas. We were selling them drip irrigation. Listening to what they are up against, the middlemen—a centuries-old system, where little cash changes hand—we had to figure out where the power resides, where the market can play a role, and where it is limited. It's not our place to judge the situation and say, 'that's wrong.' We listen, and then decide where to put our efforts."

Other gaps are internal differences in priority and approach that produce multiple, ongoing right fights within the organization. For example, there is a tension between the global portfolio managers, some of whom are based in New York, and the local relationship managers, who support the investments on a day-to-day basis. Working to identify global best practices, the New York portfolio teams seek to share insights and ideas of what works with the internal team and with external stakeholders, while the portfolio managers in the country offices are focused relentlessly on the success of the individual investments that they support. But the matrix organization that results is complex, and conflict is an inevitable—and invaluable—part of the decision-making process.

Novogratz notes, "Some of the biggest mistakes that happen are when we don't fight. People can be so nice to each other. We have a devil's advocate process where the portfolio team gets together and their job is to pressure test a potential investment so that we can look at the weaknesses before we spend too much time on due diligence. Those sessions have to be safe, but need to be really tough and contentious for us to get the maximum advantage out of them."

This structure creates an ongoing set of mutual tensions, based on team members' deep respect for each other and for their diversity of views. Over time this can be exhausting, so Novogratz and her leadership team have to pay special attention to people's pace and watch for signs of burnout. But given the stakes they are playing for, it's worth it.

Because the fund works to achieve specific goals with other nonprofits, with small- to medium-sized for-profit companies that need capital, and with large companies, decision-making strategies are fluid and tensions can escalate across the diverse landscape.

"Acumen is creating a culture where there is little or no blame," says Novogratz. "Everyone stays focused on the opportunities. I enjoy these tensions. This is part of the human

journey and it excites me." Novogratz stresses the importance
of working out tensions through relationships rather than
structures. "We don't pitch people against each other, but we
do have a diverse portfolio team. We have different world-
views that have to come into balance. Investments have to be
vetted by a diverse group."

Under Novogratz's leadership, Acumen has built an organization that depends on right fights to make right decisions.
Acumen structures its fights formally with specific processes
for application, investigation, and review. But the tensions
around conflicts and decision points work themselves out informally, both inside in the negotiations of the organization's
investment committee and outside in its flexible approaches to
implementing programs on the ground. And in a way that is
exemplary in the global world of nonprofits, Acumen relies on
an informal knowledge base, encouraging ideas that bubble
up through the hierarchy to challenge conventional wisdom.

THE UNILEVER AND Acumen stories reveal that right fights
tend to be sources of energy for transparent corporate cultures with healthy informal networks. In such environments,
structural trust is sufficient but not suffocating and levels of
personal and expertise trust are high. Conflicts focus attention on points of misalignment, competing functional biases,
and opposing views on direction and strategy, but these are
objective, structural issues that can be resolved, not subjective, irreconcilable arguments over positions and personalities. When people turn to their personal trust relationships

and expert knowledge networks for tools to work through the conflicts, the tensions actually serve to help the organization as a whole.

Leaders who learn to identify and exploit structural gaps, build personal trust relationships, and develop rich informal information networks will find those skills useful in multiple contexts. "Structure formally, but work informally" is not only a Right Fight Discipline Principle, it's a good descriptor of the way things usually work in the highest-functioning organizations we know.

NINE

Right Fight Principle #6: Turn Pain into Gain

IN THE LAST chapter, we looked at two worldwide organizations—corporate giant Unilever and the nonprofit Acumen Fund—and discovered that for both entities, tensions around decision points and structural transitions actually help energize and renew their executives and employees. This probably seems counterintuitive. Most of us associate conflict and tension not with energy and enthusiasm but with frustration, exhaustion, and burnout.

Right-fight wisdom makes all the difference when it comes to how people feel about the conflicts they're involved in. Part of the reason Vindi Banga and Jacqueline Novogratz find energy where most of us see only drain is that they have mastered the first two Right Fight Discipline Principles: they locate conflict at places of structural misalignment, tapping personal and expertise resources in the informal organization to address it, *and* they referee among diverse perspectives according to understood rules and boundaries.

Following the "make it sport, not war" and "structure formally but work informally" rules is usually enough to keep conflicts from robbing an organization of its vitality and momentum. But to truly release the energy of conflict in positive ways, leaders have to master the third rule of right fights as well. They have to find ways to turn pain into gain for themselves and their teams.

The "pain into gain" principle requires leaders to focus squarely on people. There is a fine line between productive tension and destructive distress, and no two people draw that line in exactly the same place. For right fights to be fought right, leaders need to make sure no one is put under unbearable pressure. Turning pain into gain requires leaders to relate to their team members as individuals and to figure out what creates energy, stretches skills, and honors outcomes for each of them.

TURN PAIN INTO GAIN—INCREASE ENERGY

At the root of our personal dislike of tension is the stress reaction. It's the familiar fight-or-flight response we all have when we face situations and events our bodies decode as somehow similar to the attack of a saber-toothed tiger. It's been a while since most of us lived in caves and had to deal with tigers, but our bodies haven't changed much. As a result, we often have strong physiological reactions to psychological situations when the most ancient portions of our brains interpret them as dangerous.

The physiological changes produced by the fight-or-flight response are very helpful when you need to fend off a tiger or shoot down a woolly mammoth—or otherwise fight for your life. Unfortunately, it turns out that our brains are not very good at distinguishing *actual* attacks on our lives from *figurative* ones. Fight-or-flight physiology is not such a good thing when "fight for your life" is a vivid metaphor rather than the literal truth.

Faced with stressful conditions that continue over time, fight-or-flight physiology can become the body's normal state. When that happens, the long-term effects are serious—and seriously bad. Almost all of the hormonal, biochemical, and neurochemical effects associated with fight-or-flight can have significant negative consequences for work habits, management skills, and the ability to cooperate well with others in an organizational setting.

So if stress is bad, how can tension be good?

As we discussed in Chapter 1, recent brain research is beginning to shed light on how this works. Dr. Paul Rosch, president of the American Institute of Stress, puts it simply: individual performance improves as stress increases—but only to a point. Past that point, performance declines precipitously and, if subjected to distress for extended periods of time, people get sick. But within an acceptable range of competition and tension, more of the brain is firing, more pathways are stimulated, and more creative centers are engaged. In short, more of what makes each of us unique, creative, and passionate is available for use. It's good for you and your brain to be pushed to "the Goldilocks amount"—not too much, and not too little.

Along the same lines, Theresa Wellbourne's research on workplace performance shows that groups have clear patterns of energy preference. Success and productivity are most likely when employees operate at an energy level that is somewhere in their high-midrange, above where they think they would feel most comfortable, but not so high as to wipe them out with continual stress.

Both organizations and individuals benefit when people find their energy sweet spots and operate out of them. But every employee reacts to stress uniquely, and each has a different stress-level preference. How can you as a leader identify the right stress level for each employee?

Put Passions to Work

First you have to accept that over the long term, personal motivation has to come from *the nature of the work itself*. It's a simple idea but easy to forget in a world where complicated incentive schemes suggest motivation can be bought. In his book *Why Pride Matters More Than Money*, Jon Katzenbach describes the distinctive traits that "master motivators" use to build pride in the work itself. Master motivators have an uncanny ability to figure out which assignments will create excitement and a strong sense of accomplishment in their employees.

Following the master motivator model means knowing

your employees very well and constantly monitoring their states of tension. You don't necessarily need to be formally scoring your team members every week, but you need to walk the halls and test the mood on a regular basis.

A large part of Vindi Banga's success at Unilever has to do with his ability to match his specific leaders to the challenges that each global product category presents. On the surface, his asking Silvia Lagnado to move from the Dove soap team to run soups and bouillons—a savory food category—didn't make much sense. Why would she leave a world-class brand team she had led to phenomenal success for one of the company's oldest and least interesting businesses?

But in fact, the move was perfect for Lagnado. The product was different and the new job was much bigger, but in some ways the challenges were the same as at Dove. Dove had been widely described as a stodgy "what your grandmother uses" brand before the "Campaign for Real Beauty," and the savory category, too, needed a serious image overhaul. Cynics described the soup and bouillon business as selling "glutamates in a box," and it wasn't going to be easy to turn things around.

Banga made the right call because he understood what made Lagnado tick, what personally motivated her, and what she was truly capable of. In the savory category, all of Lagnado's marketing genius was put to the test, and she found the situation totally exhilarating. Lightning struck twice, and the savory business started to grow under Lagnado's leadership after a long period of decline.

For Banga, making the right calls about his executives is

not a matter of chance. He has a genius for matching challenges to individual passions and temperament. Alan Jope,
whom Banga tapped to run Unilever Spreads and Dressings,
is a health fanatic and an intense personality. He is excited
by the challenge of making margarines and mayonnaise heart-
healthy while managing costs and competing with the bio-
fuels industry for raw materials. Peter ter Kulve, the senior
vice president of the ice cream business, is never without a
smile, is fascinated by cultural differences, and is passionate
about bringing the fun of special treats to children around the
world.

Lagnado, Jope, and ter Kulve were all relatively young
and inexperienced when Vindi Banga placed them in their
global roles. All three found the transitions uncomfortable if
not a little painful. All their businesses faced serious competitive challenges, and complacency would clearly result in
disappointing performance. But all three of them were successful because Banga recognized their personal passions and
gave them assignments where their passions could energize
their work.

TURN PAIN INTO GAIN—STRETCH SKILLS

Motivating your people to take on the right fight involves more
than knowing their passions and preferences. It also takes a
realistic understanding of their current and potential capabilities. In our work with exemplary leaders one thing is clear:
people overwhelmingly prefer a boss who challenges them to

one who sets low expectations. The trick is to figure out how to set the bar high enough to require people to stretch, but not so high that they have no hope of clearing it.

Knowing your people is the first step in setting the bar. Adopting the "never empty, never full" attitude also keeps performance tension productive. "Never empty, never full" means that, no matter how badly people fail the first time, it's not the end of the world. And no matter how well they do, there's always some room for improvement. Lagnado's success at Dove was followed by an equally impressive performance in foods because Banga kept the pressure up and didn't let her rest too comfortably on her laurels.

A third important lesson in stretching comes from the world of strategy. Before his untimely death in 2006, we had the opportunity to work with Nathaniel Mass. Nat was a positively brilliant strategist. He had an insatiable curiosity, and it led him to a diverse and distinguished professional career. He spent years at ExxonMobil, then Exxon Chemicals; went off to buy, run, and sell half a dozen businesses; became a close advisor to the leadership team at Procter & Gamble; founded the business dynamics practice at McKinsey & Company; ran a private equity fund for Monitor Consulting; and founded his own consulting firm, among other ventures.

Nat's ability to understand the essence of complex problems was outstanding. But his advice was eminently practical. When advising clients on growth strategy, he had a few simple rules. He distilled the challenge of growth into two patterns of right fights. You could sell existing products to new customers, or you could develop new capabilities to sell to your existing customers. But most of the time, when companies tried to develop new capabilities to reach new customers, they were highly likely to fail. It was just too much of a stretch.

The analogy to personal growth is highly relevant. Leaders looking to stretch skills can either ask their people to develop new capabilities in their existing environments or they can bring people with proven capabilities into new environments. But the pain is likely to exceed the potential gain when you ask people to develop new capabilities at the same time you expect them to adapt to new environments.

When Charlie Feld set out to transform the railroad he brought lots of capability in with him. The professionals he asked to build the customer service systems at Burlington Northern had proven track records of creating similar systems at least twice, and sometimes three times, in their careers. But none of them had ever worked for a railroad, so the stretch was to apply what they knew in a different environment.

When Julie Taymor was given the job to direct *The Lion King* on Broadway, she made a similar move. The first person she hired on her team was Michael Curry. Taymor needed Curry's technical genius to create the mechanics behind the hundreds of puppets she envisioned to bring the Disney tale to life on stage. Curry had successfully collaborated with Taymor in film and in her opera productions of *Oedipus Rex* and *The Magic Flute*, but he had never worked on Broadway. In fact, many of the key players on Taymor's production team were new to the Great White Way. Like Feld, Taymor stretched her technical experts by asking them to transfer their distinctive skills to a new environment.

Taymor's *The Lion King* also stretched people very familiar with the Broadway stage to develop new skills. Max Casella and Tom Alan Robbins, who originated the parts of Timon and Pumba, were veteran actors with multiple film and stage credits under their belts. But neither had any experience with the puppets that were critical to their roles.

None of this was easy for the professionals involved. Roger Allers, the film's codirector, points out that "musicals are tough. They are a hard form to do well. Modern audiences have lost touch with the conventions of slipping in and out of fantasy that musicals demand." As Taymor describes in her book *The Lion King: Pride Rock on Broadway* (Disney, 1998):

> Watching the actors rehearse with the puppets, I saw their potential, but I worried. . . . Would the puppetry interfere with telling the story? But whenever one of the actors began to master the form, I felt the tremendous emotion that a puppet or mask can communicate. I watched Scar and knew that a human being alone could not achieve the same visual power without the mask. The interplay between the performer and his extended animal character was new and exciting.

Taymor calculated the risks she was taking each step along the way. But the growing pains her team experienced turned into gains measured in Tony Awards, critical acclaim, and tremendous box office receipts, transforming *The Lion King* from kids' cartoon into groundbreaking, breathtaking live theater.

TURN PAIN INTO GAIN—
HONOR ALL OUTCOMES

In every fight, there are winners and losers. Not all ideas are good ones, and not all strategies work. And communicating the outcome to the loser can be hard. It's not easy to give people bad news without damaging personal relationships.

Difficult Conversations by Douglas Stone, Bruce Patton, and Sheila Heen (Viking, 1999) is a good place to start if you want to develop your skills in this area. Such skills are well worth developing, because how people feel about conflict after it is resolved is often determined largely by what happens to the *losers.*

To represent the mystical nature of *The Lion King*'s primate shaman, Rafiki, scenic designer Richard Hudson created a special set piece—a magical hemisphere, emerging dramatically from behind a tree. But Tsidii Le Loka, the South African actress who brought Rafiki to life, so engaged the group with improvised Zulu stories at an early workshop that Taymor decided to simplify the scene and focus all attention on her. Hudson fought to keep the globe in the set, but Taymor took it out anyway. The designer lamented the loss, saying, "It was textured, and beautiful, and expensive, and it was cut."

Taymor persuaded Hudson to see things her way, and the rich rewards of working on such a unique and innovative show more than outweighed for him the pain of losing this one battle. Besides, in this case the "loser" ended up with a Tony Award, a Critics Circle Design Award, an Ovation Award, and the Hollywood NAACP Award for Best Set Design. The story of Hudson's globe is an extreme case, but it demonstrates an important point about turning pain into gain.

Like Taymor with Hudson, wise leaders position those who lose right fights so that they have opportunities for later, greater success. When a right fight is fought right, every option has strong advocates. All propositions are well defended. Lots of very good ideas—and even some great ones—get put on the table. At the end of the day, only one position prevails. But everyone should feel rewarded for his or her efforts.

This is not to say you should create a culture of mediocrity where everyone always feels like a winner. We all know this doesn't work. But when people deliver results and fight right fights to the best of their abilities, they should gain something real and valuable even when they find themselves on the losing side. To get people to step up and take risks, you have to reward risk taking itself, not just successful outcomes.

We looked at Jack Welch's highly publicized three-way horse race to name his successor at GE in Chapter 1. Were Bob Nardelli and Jim McNerney happy when Jeff Immelt got the job? Probably not. They reacted well in public though they were, of course, privately disappointed. But Welch had been upfront from the beginning that there was only one CEO spot at GE, and he kept his promise to see that all three men made successful transitions to the chief executive's office somewhere. Following their six-month trial by fire at GE, Nardelli and Mc-Nerney went on to the top jobs at 3M and Home Depot.

Of course, leaders don't usually have the option of sending their right fight losers on to Tony Awards and CEO positions.

But gain for the loser doesn't have to be glorious. It just has to be good enough.

Consider Rolf Classon's handling of the executive who lost the opportunity to run the proposed new business. Classon set up his right fight so that lots of voices were heard, from both inside and outside the company, and in the end, the majority of voices said that the acquisition just didn't fit the company's overall strategy. The disappointed executive went on to run another division within the company, so no one could interpret his loss in the acquisition battle as a vote of no confidence in his abilities or leadership. It wasn't the outcome he wanted, but Classon made sure it was an outcome he gained from.

Executives who engage in right fights constantly balance the tension between what's good for their team members' personal growth and what's good for the company as a whole. Like the U.S. Marine Corps's dual mission statement, great leaders will absolutely accomplish their objectives, and they will take care of each and every one of their people.

CASE STUDY: *BMC Rationalizes Its Sales Force*

- **Increase Energy**—An organizational refocus released enormous energy and growth in a business everyone had written off.
- **Stretch Skills**—Could a former army product engineer really run a mainframe sales force?
- **Honor Outcomes**—Giving one high-profile executive a plum assignment can cause problems when there's not another plum.

When Bob Beauchamp took the CEO reins at BMC Software, he knew he was sitting on a time bomb. He had a mainframe utilities business that generated very attractive margins, but zero growth. He had a strong vision for building a new growth business around business service management (BSM), but whether he could grow it fast enough to offset the ongoing decline in demand for mainframes was a question mark.

For years, BMC had sold its entire product line to customers through a single enterprise sales force. In the race to build the new business service management business, BMC bought over forty companies between 2000 and 2007. One of the benefits of buying all these smaller software companies was that BMC could immediately increase sales by offering new products to their existing customers.

But this strategy didn't work well in practice. Sales reps continued to move the products they were most familiar with, and margins went down on most of the newly acquired product lines. In spite of their best efforts, Beauchamp and the sales team sweated every quarter, and on two occasions missed their numbers, causing the stock to plummet.

To turn things around, Beauchamp pulled all the classic levers. He eliminated underperforming products and rationalized the overall product portfolio. To take out costs, he centralized as many functions as he could and dramatically streamlined all aspects of the organization—except the field sales force. With margins down, BMC's only hope was to keep revenues up.

But in spite of all the efforts of Beauchamp and his team, the mainframe business continued to reflect the global decline in overall market demand, and the growth of new BSM business wasn't sufficient to make up for the declines in the mainframe markets. The threat of posting lackluster numbers continued.

Bill Miller, the manager of the mainframe product group, had argued for his own dedicated sales force for years. He knew intuitively that unless he could get a small group of reps to focus on the increasingly specialized mainframe market, he would be relegated to managing a declining product portfolio. Margins remained high on the mainframe side, but all the cash was going to Miller's colleague Jim Grant to invest in the BSM growth business.

BMC executives had long debated the merits of a unified sales force with one point of customer contact. Customers liked using their purchasing clout to get mainframe tools at steep discounts in exchange for buying BMC's new products, but the sales deals reduced margins. There were already dozens of mainframe product specialists in the field, and it would increase costs to separate out mainframe sales as well. And though Miller was a solid product VP, some wondered if he could run a stand-alone business unit.

But Beauchamp realized that Miller deserved a stretch opportunity. In a survey of the top 150 leaders at BMC, he had emerged as one of three executives that people throughout the organization looked up to on all dimensions. He was trustworthy, had deep expertise in his markets and products, and was good to work for—tough but fair.

In addition, Beauchamp knew he had to do something to stem the continuing decline on the mainframe side of the house. He understood that executives up and down the line in the mainframe division were weary of trying to wrestle precious sales time and energy from a field sales force trained to pitch the next shiny object. Motivation levels in the division were declining, and the company was at risk of losing some of its best mainframe engineers.

There were two key questions for Beauchamp as he considered yet another shakeup in BMC's organizational structure. The first was how to treat Jim Grant fairly if he gave Miller his own business. Grant, too, was a highly admired leader both internally and externally. He was bound to be unhappy if Miller was handed a P&L and he wasn't. The second question for Beauchamp was how to keep BMC together and under his leadership if he spun both mainframes and BSM into their own separate units.

After much heated debate, Beauchamp decided to give Miller the sales team he was asking for. With the addition of sales, mainframes became more or less a business unit, with Miller at the helm. Grant got control of all BMC's remaining products and product lines, consolidated into his BSM growth business. The product division was still a cost center, but product marketing was added to Grant's portfolio of responsibilities, giving him some amount of leverage when dealing with the corporate sales force.

Results of the reorg were almost immediate. After years of small but steady declines in revenue, the newly created mainframe sales team, spurred on by Miller, generated double-digit growth in its first two years. Already high, margins for mainframes improved significantly once the practice of discounting mainframe products in order to close new BSM license revenue was held in check.

The BSM business grew, too. Without the safety net of mainframe maintenance revenues to fall back on, the growth sales team had to step up their efforts. Not everyone was happy about it, of course. Many products had been eliminated when Beauchamp rationalized the portfolio, and losing the mainframe business as well meant that sales had to generate more revenue from a much smaller product line. But the sales group's former complacency was replaced by a real passion to grow the new business and demonstrate that it could be run at decent margins. And Grant leveraged his marketing authority to put pressure on the field organization to open new channels and improve cost performance.

The stock tripled; Miller was happy; and Grant, who had argued for a deal similar to Miller's and lost, ended up happy, too. Running the new growth part of the business with its expanded marketing functions proved exciting, and the expanded job allowed Grant to keep living in his beloved California instead of forcing him to locate near BMC's Texas headquarters.

Bob Beauchamp was able to balance the competing individual needs of his executive team members against the larger interests of BMC's future business strategy. Stretching Bill Miller to lead the mainframe business not only offered him a long-sought personal growth opportunity, it revitalized the entire mainframe business. By focusing sales energies externally instead of internally—on customer needs instead of maintaining mainframe discounts—the formerly moribund division saw dramatic improvements in growth and margins.

Stretching Jim Grant to manage all product lines and product marketing also had positive impact on both him and his team. Forced to rely on their own resources for cash to grow the BSM business, the growth team found ways to reduce costs, increase sales, and improve margins. Beauchamp's right fight turned pain into gain across the board at BMC.

Balancing the need to develop your people against the demands of day-to-day business priorities isn't easy in any business. When you run what is arguably the most people intensive business in the world, the oldest strategy consulting firm, these trade-offs will be at the core of your success or failure.

CASE STUDY: *McKinsey & Company Recruits Right Fighters*

- **Increase energy**—Who gets complacent in an up-or-out culture?
- **Stretch skills**—McKinsey hires the top talent and puts them under pressure to grow into new roles every two to three years.
- **Honor outcomes**—While most people leave the firm, the alumni network is extensive and is an enviable asset for business development.

Several years ago an article that appeared in *The Economist* made a bold claim. The article asserted that only two large institutions consistently turn out top business leaders—

GE and McKinsey & Company. While much has been written about GE, inside insight into McKinsey is much more difficult to find.

Although management consulting goes in and out of favor among graduates of the world's top business schools, McKinsey's ability to attract and develop the best and brightest business minds is remarkable.

This is particularly true if you know the odds. Less than one in five new McKinsey hires will ever make partner, and less than one in ten will go on to become a director in the firm. And the firm as an organization is an unusual pyramid of energy and raw talent. At any point in time, half of the employees have less than two years experience in consulting, and less than a third of its professionals have more than two years experience in their current job.

So how does McKinsey earn its international reputation for expertise? Complex knowledge management systems? Proprietary research? Not really. McKinsey's success is due to a simple development tension: up or out.

The firm's people development group would be the first to admit that the system works on apprenticeship and pressure. New associates enter with the common but unspoken expectation that they will be "counseled out" at the end of the first review cycle. They also expect to learn more in one year at McKinsey than they could in several years anywhere else.

The way the development system works is remarkably simple. New associates are eager to prove themselves on their first assignments and work hard to demonstrate basic consulting skills and pick up industry knowledge on the way. Subsequent assignments allow them to build on the basics and expand their expertise with different clients or in different parts of the same client organization. Associates are promoted to managers and managers to associate principals to further stretch their development.

McKinsey works by throwing people into situations that are a little over their heads, giving them enough senior coverage that they won't embarrass themselves or the firm, and then expecting them to fill in the gaps for themselves. McKinsey's people stretch because they have to, and both the consultants and the organization benefit in the process. The result of the system is that everyone grows, even though very few win the coveted partner's position.

The reality is that fewer than 20 percent of the firm's employees are asked to exit the firm. Most who go leave for better opportunities, to run something, or to decrease their travel load and improve their lifestyle. This voluntary up or out works in the firm's favor as well. Ex-McKinsey consultants sit in important positions at companies that are also clients of the firm. One of the most productive ways for a McKinsey consultant to get an introduction to a potential new client is for him or her to search the alumni database.

An interesting test of McKinsey's up-or-out paradigm happened during the dot-com bust a few years ago. In one year, the firm's acceptance rates from business schools went from 40 percent to 90 percent. Recruiting was at an all time high at the same time demand for work was dropping off. There were far too many new associates and far too few assignments for them to work on.

The firm did what any business would do—it shed 40 percent of the incoming associate class. The internal party line was that McKinsey had become lax about hiring and was returning to its long established meritocracy policy—that the firm had lost its values in the dot-com boom and was simply restoring them and returning to its usual practices.

Unfortunately what looked like a layoff and felt like a layoff was hard to describe to the people affected as a return to values. Many associates were shunted back into a tough job market after only six to nine months at the firm, never having had any significant engagement experience where they could prove themselves. There just wasn't enough opportunity to go around.

For the first time in decades, McKinsey's vaunted development strategy hadn't worked for a large group of alumni. Denied a fair shot and flung back into the market without good alternatives, many of the associates were bitter about McKinsey's aberration from its usual practices. They had been promised right fight opportunities, and they ended up in a very wrong scenario. The firm continues to this day to struggle to rebuild goodwill with that generation of leaders.

McKinsey's experience with the dot-com class reveals a lot about right fights and how people respond to them. By any measure, the up-or-out culture at the firm is stressful and demanding. Most people leave within a few years of joining, but unlike the unfortunate victims of the dot-com debacle, very few regard the time they spent at McKinsey as wasted. Most alumni look back on their McKinsey experience as a period of combined personal discovery and professional development.

The reason is pretty simple. When it operates properly, McKinsey's culture functions like an ongoing master class in how to find right fights and fight them right.

For McKinsey consultants, the experience of working in the firm undeniably matters. Focus on the future is a given, because staying in one place is virtually impossible. And the purpose is noble. McKinsey may not always fulfill its own values, but the values themselves are worthwhile.

McKinsey's development system has clear rules, mentors who referee, and a playing field that is the same for everybody. The demands may be stressful, but it's sport, not war. While the formal structure of the firm is both clear and hierarchical, the development of extensive personal and professional networks is encouraged and supported. And we just looked at how the up-or-out paradigm increases energy levels, stretches skills, and usually works so that pain turns into gain in the long run.

McKinsey recruits vast numbers of people into training for right fights by promising that the knowledge and experience they'll gain will make the struggle worth it, win or lose. Good leaders can take a page from McKinsey's playbook. Positioning people in true right fights and showing them how to fight the fights right develops them in countless ways and prepares them to become leaders themselves.

TEN

Conclusion

GOOD LEADERS ASK themselves, "What is the purpose of this organization? How can we do the job better?"

But *great* leaders ask themselves, "How can I push this organization to find its top performance and purpose? Where do I need to inject tension to get the best out of everyone? *What needs to change?*"

Organizations have always thrived on tension, but today, with global interdependence, giant matrix organizations, and a relentlessly rapid pace, the need for creative tension is greater than ever.

It's the leaders at the top and in the middle who must set the course, create alignment around the essential goals of the organization, and then figure out where to animate tension to make the organization really hum. Great leaders are able to use all six of the Right Fight Principles to create the right tensions in their organizations and keep them functioning at peak level. Great leaders help their organizations fight the right fights.

Moreover, the only way for great leaders to find and develop leaders for the future is to test them in right fights. It's in the crucible of productive tension that great leaders are created.

RIGHT FIGHTS AS MODEL

Julie Taymor, Rolf Classon, LaVerne Council, Doug Conant, Jacqueline Novogratz, Vindi Banga, and Charlie Feld all have this in common as great leaders. They possess an amazing combination of personal and professional traits that transcend the arenas in which they are famous—the arts, public policy, and business. They are at once storytellers, show people, scavengers, and straddlers.

As storytellers, they share the ability to capture the essence of a situation and communicate it in powerfully simple ways—to cast the kind of vision that opens tight corporate budgets and rallies beleaguered troops. This ability to influence and inspire while getting to the heart of the matter is essential to setting up right fights effectively, because convincing others to come along on a bumpy ride is a critical component of success.

Being a showman or showwoman means more than being comfortable in the public eye. It also means being willing to audition, to try out, to risk change in order to make things better. Like all great performers, great leaders are big on experiments, pilots, and tests. They ground themselves in results they can measure, because investigating whether or not things will actually *work* is one of the most effective ways to sort through competing alternatives.

Great leaders are often called visionary, and they do cast compelling visions for others to follow. But if you look more closely, you find that they actually assimilate and integrate far more than they create from scratch. They study their circumstances, using past experience to serve present needs. Scavengers of good ideas from a broad range of sources, these leaders look for wisdom anywhere they can find it.

But if there is any one characteristic that distinguishes the best of the best in leaders, it's their ability to work at multiple levels at the same time. They create compelling visions of the future, but aren't afraid to dive deeply into the details of how to make those visions a reality. This ability to straddle the gap between vision and execution is an important key to working through tension on a practical level.

Basically, great leaders internalize right-fight wisdom. The six principles we've explored in this book are part of their DNA, their working norm. As a result, they can creatively use the energy inherent in tension to get the best from their people and their organizations. Consistently, great leaders choose the right fights and fight them right.

RIGHT FIGHTS AS STRATEGY

Business schools, management books, and training programs don't teach leaders how to do this. You don't have to look far to see the evidence. There are wrong fights everywhere, in organizations of all shapes and sizes.

Focusing on the past, stigmatizing the losers, fighting over turf—it's easy to see the negative side of tension. But without tension, nothing moves. It's friction that holds things together while they're moving and keeps systems from flying apart. What matters is making tension work for you in positive ways.

To make tension positive, the real trick is to *systematize* right fighting. Following the Right Fight Principles has cumulative force. Observing one Right Fight Principle—say, focusing on the future—can help everyone stop bickering about the past and start paying attention to things that matter *now*. But the fight over *now* can still go wrong if people focus on the turf they hope to control in the future rather than something that matters, like products or customers.

It helps to combine several of the Right Fight Principles to ensure your right fight is set up to succeed. Focus on the future, and while you're doing that be sure there's also a higher purpose and some way for everyone to grow or gain from the pain. The more right fight wisdom you apply, the more you call up the extraordinary strength of an organizational culture that does most things right. Such cultures become self-sustaining because people want to work in energizing, nontoxic environments.

RIGHT FIGHTS AS DISCIPLINE

No one masters right fights once and for all. Memorizing the principles doesn't guarantee that everything will work out perfectly ever after. Even McKinsey & Company, whose associate development process models right fighting as well as anything we've ever seen, hasn't always managed to implement that process successfully in real-world situations.

Right fights move as organizations mature and circumstances change. The future slides into the past, misalignments get lined up, informal networks become hierarchical structures. What's a right fight today can easily turn into a wrong fight tomorrow if the ground shifts, the rules are rewritten, or the stakes change.

Adopting right fight wisdom as a discipline will help you stay centered when things around you are in flux. Examine each new situation with the Right Fight Principles in mind, and you'll be able to sort out what's worth fighting over and what needs to be quickly resolved. Apply the Right Fight Discipline Principles intentionally and thoughtfully, and you'll keep the right fights you do decide to wage from degenerating into exhausting battles without benefits.

The successful leaders we've profiled don't use Right Fight Principles as a method of last resort, but as their usual method of approaching people and problems. They've embraced right fighting as a discipline, and the results speak for themselves.

RIGHT FIGHTS AS TOOLS

Some of the leaders whose stories we've told in this book were born with right fight talent. Their DNA fortuitously encodes the ability to feel jazzed when the pressure is on and to communicate their energy to those around them. Others developed their skill sets more painfully over time by the process of trial and error.

What excites us, though, is that anyone can learn what Charlie Feld or Jacqueline Novogratz or Vindi Banga knows instinctively. Tension creates energy. Energy motivates people. People make things happen. And the things that happen will be good if the energy that drives them is moving in positive ways through productive channels.

So take this book and use it. Ask yourself: what are the tensions, the fights, the struggles I am facing? Are they with myself? In my family? In my community? In my organization? In my artistic and spiritual life?

No matter where you find a struggle, right fight wisdom applies. In this book we've looked at right fights everywhere from the backstage of Broadway to the back roads of rural India, from the boardrooms of corporate giants to the bond battles of suburban school districts, and from the "Campaign for Real Beauty" to the fall of the Berlin Wall.

If you take away anything from all we've shown you, take this: anywhere tension exists, the opportunity to make it work *for* you rather than against you exists, too.

For each fight you find, ask yourself: is this a right fight? Let the Right Fight Principles be your starting point. Does this struggle matter? Is it focused on the future and not the past? Is there a higher, noble purpose to be served?

If the answer to these questions is yes, then you're ready to move confidently forward. If the answer is no, you have two choices. One is to commit yourself to study the Right Fight Principles and transform the conflict so that it is a right fight.

The other is to stop it cold, replacing the battle with something more worthy of your time, passions, and efforts.

When you know your fight is a right one, use the right fight rules to guide your actions. Make it sport, not war, and be sure all involved know the rules, the referee, and the boundary lines of the playing field. Structure formally but work informally, utilizing the full resources of your personal and information networks. Turn the pain into gain for yourself and those around you. Use your right fight to increase energy, stretch skills, and position people for future success.

Bring this book to your meetings, and ask your teams to do the same. There is great benefit in synergy, and it helps tremendously when right fight discipline becomes the norm across an organization. While it is hard (sometimes *very* hard), you will be amazed at how productive and satisfying the process is. And you will discover amazing qualities in those around you that you were completely unaware of at the start.

Right-fight wisdom works, and now is the time to embrace it. The stakes are high, perhaps never higher. What will improve economic outcomes for the world's citizens but still protect the increasingly endangered and fragile global environment? How do we honor diverse cultures and preferences in an ever more interconnected and demanding world? Can we balance urgent needs against the obligation to consider consequences?

We need better answers, more innovations, and diverse options. The energy we need to solve our biggest problems exists. Right now it's potential energy and it's is locked up in the tensions in and around those problems. Activating that energy and releasing it in productive ways will unleash an unprecedented amount of human potential. Be a part of that process. Master the right fights.

Part FOUR

TOOLS: TESTS *for* IDENTIFYING *and* LEADING RIGHT FIGHTS

Is the Challenge Worth a Right Fight? Right Fight Decision Principles—Assessment Tool

OUR FIRST THREE principles provide a straightforward way to determine whether you have a goal or objective that's worthy of a right fight. This assessment walks you through those principles systematically to help you determine if an issue you are currently facing is an appropriate candidate.

With the specific challenge, issue, or goal that you would like to test in mind, ask yourself the following questions. The more specific you can be about stating the challenge, the more helpful the answers to the questions will be in determining whether you have the makings of a successful right fight.

1. THE MATERIALITY PRINCIPLE

Make It Material—The Value Test

Could you . . . ?

1. Save 15 percent or more of your resources or time for a year or longer?
2. Charge 10 percent or more than you do today?
3. Grow your sales or share of customers faster than the market is growing?
4. Lower the risks to the organization substantially?

If the answer to one or more of these questions is "yes," the challenge passes the value test.

If the answer to all four was "no," the challenge isn't big enough to make it worthy of a right fight. You have two choices. You can either restate the challenge in much bolder terms or use the traditional tools of alignment to deal with this particular issue.

Make It Material—The Thinking Test

Can you solve the challenge by . . . ?

5. Relying on routine processes and common skills in your organization?
6. Calling in an expert to solve it for you?
7. Breaking it up into smaller issues or tasks and coordinating progress between the various smaller efforts?

8. Appointing a single leader to drive to an acceptable answer?

9. Holding different people or parts of your organization accountable for their separate pieces of the problem?

If the answer to one or more of these questions is "yes," the challenge probably isn't complex enough to pass the thinking test. If you can get to a good enough solution by routine delegation or hiring outside expertise, tension is likely to get in the way.

To successfully pass the thinking test, the answer to one or more of the following questions has to be "yes":

10. Does the issue require careful balancing of multiple perspectives to arrive at a best answer?

11. Do different parts of your team or organization need to do *real work together* to arrive at a solution?

12. Does a good solution require different people to lead the process at different times?

13. Does a good solution require mutual accountability for the answer?

One or more "yes" answers on questions 10 through 13 suggest the challenge falls squarely in the domain of exponential, out-of-the box thinking and requires careful balancing of different views and perspectives. That makes for a right fight.

If the challenge passes the value test, but doesn't pass the thinking test, you're probably much better off not wasting the time and energy required to pull off a successful right fight.

Issues that can be settled routinely should be, no matter how large or potentially valuable they are.

Make It Material—The Change Test
Will the solution require . . . ?

14. The organization to work in a fundamentally different way?
15. A new way to integrate big-picture organizational perspectives with specialized local knowledge?
16. New real-time information flow between different parts of the organization?

If the answer to one or more of these questions is "yes," the challenge is likely to pass the change test. There is a subtle but important difference between a potential right fight and a critical task-force exercise. The result of a material fight should be a noticeable difference in the way an organization works.

If the answer to all three of the last questions was "no," you may have a very interesting team problem-solving challenge, but you are unlikely to have the makings of a material right fight.

2. FUTURE FOCUS PRINCIPLE
Focus on the Future—The Possibility Test
Is the challenge about . . . ?

17. Sorting out the details of what happened in the past?

18. Determining blame or accountability for the organization's current circumstances?

A "yes" answer to either of these questions is a red flag for the possibility test. Remember that no amount of debate can truly change the answer to empirical questions. Adversarial debate is an essential feature of many systems that aim at resolving questions of fact—scientific peer review and the U.S. legal system, to name a couple—but right fights should speak to what is possible, not to what is past.

To pass the possibility test, you should be looking for an answer to one of the following questions:

19. How do we avoid the mistakes of the past and improve current circumstances?
20. Which course of action creates greater possibility for success?
21. What is the best way to turn a future vision into reality?

Focus on the Future—The Compelling Test
Does the possibility . . . ?

22. Require significant innovations, some of which may not be invented yet?
23. Create a future vision that is exciting enough to get people to take real risks?
24. Promise a future that is so much better than today that people are willing to change?

If you answer "yes" to one or more of the last three questions, the challenge meets the compelling test. The challenge has the potential to focus people so intently on real, achievable benefits that they are willing to work through the costs and controversies associated with waging a successful right fight.

Focus on the Future—The Uncertainty Test
Does the solution . . . ?

25. Require you to respond to unpredictable, wild-card uncertainties like changes in regulation or dramatic shifts in the economy?
26. Demand response to competitive uncertainties: unexpected changes in customer preferences, disruptive changes in technologies, or channel shifts?
27. Present difficult internal choices where the best way forward is not clear? (For example, past history is not helpful, or potential costs and benefits compete.)

If you answer "yes" to one or more of the last three questions, the challenge meets the uncertainty test. Remember: if the way forward is clear, debate will just slow you down.

In order to qualify as a right fight, your challenge has to have all three elements of the future focus principle. It must unearth new possibilities, paint a compelling vision of the future to come, and require the navigation of real uncertainty.

3. THE NOBLE PURPOSE PRINCIPLE

Pursuing a Noble Purpose—The Intangibility Test

Does the challenge . . . ?

28. Speak to more than making money?
29. Reflect a larger cause that is central to your organization's mission statement or purpose?
30. Flow directly from the values of the organization?

If the answer to one or more of the last three questions is "yes," there is a high probability that the challenge can be expressed in terms that will give people a sense of greater purpose.

If the answers to all three of the above questions are "no," you should think about whether there is an opportunity to translate a mundane objective like saving money into a more noble one like making your products more affordable to your customers, thereby improving their lives. Right fights are rarely successful unless people can see some kind of intangible benefit.

Pursuing a Noble Purpose—The Energizing Test

Will the process of solving the challenge . . . ?

31. Motivate people in your group or organization to go above and beyond their ordinary responsibilities?
32. Translate into statements or actions that can be embraced by employees from the top to the bottom of the organization?

33. Seem important enough that people are willing to dissent?
34. Encourage people to put aside their differences and individual priorities in order to create a better outcome for the organization as a whole?
35. Instill pride throughout the organization?

The more "yes" answers you can create to the energizing test, the more likely it is that people up and down the organization will work to find the best answer possible. Over the long term, tension requires energy focused around a cause worth fighting for to be productive.

Pursuing a Noble Purpose—The Respect Test
Will the solution . . . ?

36. Win respect and admiration from stakeholders outside the organization?
37. Produce outcomes that the average worker will be willing to bring up in conversations with friends and neighbors?
38. Generate positive external press or recognition for the group?
39. Encourage people outside the organization to support your efforts no matter how difficult or painful they may be?
40. Win the respect of your opponents or competitors?

If you answered "yes" to one or more of these questions then you have all the necessary ingredients for a noble purpose. And if you've gotten this far, your challenge has all the makings of a right fight—material, visionary, and related to a purpose larger than the organization itself.

It may seem like a very high bar for any challenge to pass all these separate tests. But tension is most productive when these elements are in place. Our research, reflected in the cases we've profiled, reveals that most right fights do in fact pass virtually all these tests.

Taking the time to work through these tests will help focus your efforts. If the issue you're testing repeatedly misses the mark, you can look to alignment or delegation as your solution and avoid unproductive conflict.

If the issue easily meets all the standards, you have confirmation that yours is a right fight. This confirmation is important, because our work with leaders around the globe shows that for any given group there can be no more than two to four right fights at any point in time. Before you try to use tension productively, you need to be sure the conditions are conducive to success.

If your intuition tells you that your challenge is indeed right-fight material, but it missed the mark on one or two dimensions, the following assessment tools will identify the areas where you need to reframe the challenge so it qualifies as a right fight. Frequently these areas involve being bolder with your aspirations, moving beyond the present to future possibilities, or linking to an energizing sense of purpose that will resonate up and down your organization.

IS THE CHALLENGE WORTH A RIGHT FIGHT?
Assessment Tool for Teams: The Prioritization Matrix

Every year we conduct dozens of top team workshops around the globe. One of the easiest and most effective ways to identify the right fights in an organization is a very simple team exercise that's proven worthwhile in large and small organizations in many cultures.

We typically do this exercise at the beginning of strategic planning workshops or team effectiveness workshops to identify the most strategic team challenges that a group will face in the not-too-distant future.

First, have your team brainstorm the top ten to twelve initiatives or strategic priorities that the group needs to address over the course of the next twelve to eighteen months.

Second, draw a simple two-by-two matrix where the vertical dimension represents future value to the organization. It's important for the group to brainstorm criteria to define "value." Most business teams come up with cost savings or equivalent improvements in net margins through new revenue streams. On the nonprofit side, the value dimension tends to be expressed in terms of impact on target communities or stakeholders—for example, improving prenatal care or bringing in a whole new generation of members to a museum or arts organization.

The horizontal dimension should reflect how organizationally complex achieving the outcome is likely to be. An initiative that can be undertaken successfully within one organizational unit is relatively low. And an initiative that requires many people or groups to contribute is relatively high on this dimension. We usually ask leaders to think of this axis as a combination of strong interest to work on a topic and belief that their contribution to the given topic will make a material difference to the outcome.

SINGLE PERSON OR GROUP TASK   MULTIPLE GROUPS OR TEAM TASK

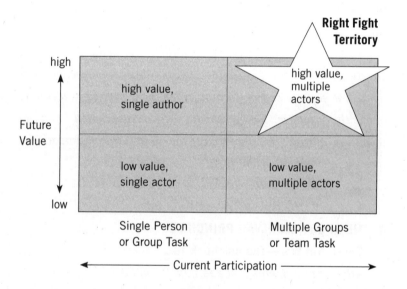

Have the group plot all ten to twelve identified initiatives within this two-by-two prioritization grid, then discuss and reconcile any significant discrepancies that occur. Once the team feels the issue list has been sorted correctly, look at the initiatives that are high value and represent high organizational challenge. In most cases you will have found the handful of right fights in the team or organization.

Is the Challenge Being Fought Right?
Right Fight Discipline Principles—Assessment Tool

Our three *Right Fight Discipline Principles* provide a framework for leaders to determine whether the conditions are in place to allow an identified right fight to be fought productively and well. These principles of engagement differ from the *Right Fight Decision Principles* in that they can rarely be expressed as objective yes or no tests. Because these principles are skill-based and subjective, these questions will require self-reflection.

To determine how well your challenge is being fought, ask yourself the following questions again, with the specific right fight that you are testing in mind. The more specific you can be about the situation, the more helpful the answers will be in determining whether you are making the most of the organizational tension inherent in a right fight.

4. THE SPORT, NOT WAR PRINCIPLE

Sport, Not War—The Rulebook Test
What are the norms that keep things on track?

41. Are there clear boundaries for conduct and behavior in the conflict?
42. Are people in the group encouraged to speak up when they have dissenting points of view?
43. Are mechanisms in place to keep debate on a professional level?

44. What happens when the conversation degenerates into personal attacks?

45. Does the group reach false consensus, then openly disagree when the debate is over?

46. Are individuals allowed or encouraged to sabotage each others' positions?

47. Does debate occur within the group or "in the halls"?

All high-performance teams have norms, spoken or unspoken. Effective groups and leaders will penalize members who act outside the accepted behavioral norms—whether they answer e-mails in meetings or create unwelcome disruptions to timelines and discussions. If your own group hasn't agreed on explicit ground rules, now is a good time to start. Write them down and post them in meetings.

Sport, Not War—The Referee Test
Who enforces the rules?

48. Is the leader neutral, or at least genuinely open to differing points of view?

49. Does the leader set clear rules to keep the debate on track, and enforce them?

50. Do some people get away with minimal effort or contribution to the group?

51. Is someone responsible for keeping the group on task?

52. Is there sufficient flexibility in meeting agendas and forums to make sure everyone is heard?

53. Does the leader create the sense that competition is fact-based and fair?

The role of the referee is critical to a right fight. It's also one of the hardest things for senior leaders to do well. It isn't reasonable to expect leaders to have no point of view on most issues. It is critical, however, that they referee the debate without noticeable bias toward their own personal perspectives.

Sport, Not War—The Level Playing Field Test
Can the best side win?

54. Does each side of the debate have a realistic chance to win or at least influence the outcome?
55. Is it clear how a decision will be reached—for example, the leader will decide, majority rules, or consensus is required?
56. Is the outcome a foregone conclusion?

Of course it's true that competitions are rarely matched in a way that's perfectly even. Each of the opposing sides has strengths and each has disadvantages. But if the competition seems like an elephant dancing with a chicken screaming "Every man for himself!" you should take a good hard look at the playing field. A fight whose outcome is a foregone conclusion is not a right fight.

5. THE STRUCTURE FORMALLY BUT WORK INFORMALLY PRINCIPLE

Structure Formally—The Exploit the Gaps Test

Is there imperfect alignment?

57. Do different parts of the group or team have different structural interests or agendas?
58. Are incentives compatible but distinct enough to give each interest a specific objective or measure to champion?
59. Do the different roles on the team create advocacy for certain positions or points of view?
60. Are differences in individual priorities likely to enhance or hinder debate?
61. Are there explicit tensions in the group that have to be managed across different leaders or subgroups?
62. Is there a clear goal but differing perspectives on how best to achieve the goal?

Remember that leaders set up right fights formally in their organizations through imperfect alignment of structural trust. Dissent and productive tension will come from these gaps in alignment. If everyone's incentives are perfectly aligned, there is likely not much room for productive debate. Too much misalignment, and you have chaos with no common goals or objectives. The skillful right fight architect will create different views about common goals through these gaps in structural trust.

Work Informally—The Rely on Relationships Test
Can you count on people?

63. Will members of the group rely on their influence with their peers as well as their authority to get things done?
64. Do the members of the group have professional respect for each other?
65. Are there sufficient levels of personal trust in the group to ensure that individuals will deliver on their commitments and behave with integrity?
66. Will opinion leaders and influence brokers throughout the organization test perspectives up and down the hierarchy?
67. Will individuals deal with conflict openly and productively, and trust that their peers will do the same?

Right fights can all too easily escalate into silo wars without the critical safety blanket provided by informal personal trust networks. If these relationships are damaged, or haven't had sufficient time to develop, it's important to create opportunities for people to do real work together. If you haven't explicitly thought about who the "network hubs" in your organization are, walk the halls and see whose names are mentioned most often.

Work Informally—The Insist on Ideas Test
How do you know what you know?

68. Are you sure you have access to unfiltered information?

69. Do you seek out second and third opinions?

70. Can you tap into networks of expertise that exist within and outside your group and organization?

71. Will good ideas from the bottom of the organization get a fair hearing before the hierarchy suppresses them?

72. Are you creating a safe space to explore new ways of approaching issues or problems, no matter how farfetched they may seem?

Formal structure and hierarchy are useful because they establish clear chains of command and authority. But they inevitably suppress incompletely formed ideas that may hold the key to successful innovation or breakthrough performance. Right fights fought right depend on informal networks of advice and expertise to surface, refine, and test ideas from top to bottom in groups and organizations.

6. THE PAIN INTO GAIN PRINCIPLE
Pain Into Gain—The Increase Energy Test
Where do you land in the stress/distress continuum?

73. Are people in the group complacent?

74. Are tension levels high enough to promote optimal performance?

75. Are people excited to come in to work on the challenges before them?

76. Do the leaders have a good sense of what their people

care about, and do they put those passions to good use in motivating performance?

77. Are people motivated by the nature of the work that they have been asked to do?

78. Do leaders take routine pulse checks of their teams and adjust goals and assignments when necessary to rebalance tension levels?

It may seem counterintuitive, but all our best research on high performing teams points to the fact that people like difficult challenges. The trick here is to balance the very fine line between productive stress and destructive distress that leads to burnout. Master motivators take the time to understand their people on an individual level, set energizing challenges, and constantly monitor the pulse of their teams.

Pain into Gain—The Stretch Skills Test
Is personal development a priority?

79. Do leaders set high expectations of each person on the team?

80. Is the development bar tailored to each individual?

81. Does the bar continue to rise after each success?

82. Are failures treated as learning experiences?

83. Are people allowed to learn new skills in the relative safety of a known environment?

84. Or, are people allowed to apply proven skills in new environments?

Remember that people are far more willing to take on a right fight when they believe they will be required to stretch. Master motivators understand their people well, set individual achievement bars, and then adopt a "never empty, never full" attitude to keep performance tensions productive.

Pain into Gain—The Honor All Outcomes Test
How do the losers feel?

85. Can the leader give people bad news without damaging personal relationships?
86. Is there dignity in losing?
87. Is risk taking rewarded, even when the outcome is not a winning one?
88. Are losers better off in the long run for having tried and failed?
89. Are outcomes communicated objectively and in terms that honor the effort everyone puts into the debate?

It should be obvious by now that leaders who both architect and referee right fights need to have strong motivation and communication skills. Objectivity, candor, and sincere appreciation for extraordinary—though unsuccessful—efforts are characteristics well worth developing. People's willingness to engage in the next right fight is largely determined by what happens to the losers.

Our principles speak directly to the qualities of leadership that are necessary to create breakthrough performance, innovation, and value in today's complex organizational landscape.

Good leaders may excel in one or more of the six principles. Great leaders consistently negotiate them all.

IS THE CHALLENGE BEING FOUGHT RIGHT?
Eye-Opening Assessment Tool for Teams:
The Reverse Fishbowl

As outside advisors to leadership teams, we often try to model or simulate effective techniques or behaviors for our clients. One well-established, effective workshop technique is the "fishbowl" when workshop leaders go up in front of a group and role-play a specific scenario to give the group ideas and techniques they can use to improve their own performance. One of the most effective tools we use with senior executive teams to help them diagnose weaknesses in their "fought right" skills is a variant on the technique we like to call the "reverse fishbowl." Here's how it works.

As experts on team dynamics, we observe a leadership team in action as they debate important agenda items or strategies—we put the team in the fishbowl. We take very careful notes detailing who said what, when it was said, how long a particular conversation took, what the group's reaction was, and so on.

When we feel we have a good sense of the group dynamic, we stop the meeting and have a conversation among ourselves but in front of the group. We assess how they are doing in relatively explicit terms. We discuss what the established norms of the group are and whether people are adhering to them. We examine the role of the leader. We note evidence we've seen of informal influence techniques and people going out on a limb and trying new things. We mention specific contributions, strengths, and weaknesses of each individual team member, including the leader. We keep our comments as objective and fact based as possible, quoting individual team members directly and reporting specific reactions from the group—"Did you see Helena roll her eyes when Hans made the point about the finance numbers being unrealistic?"

The reaction we get across business groups and cultures is amazing in its consistency. We almost always do the exercise as a surprise, so there is inevitably shocked silence. But soon the silence gives way to relief, laughter, and good-natured agreement. By objectively calling out the elephants in the room, we are usually able to give people permission to try new behaviors with their peers. Invariably, after one of these sessions, quiet people will speak up, someone new will take pen to a flip chart, individuals will catch themselves in behavior quirks, and everyone will have a good laugh. But the meeting is almost always more productive.

We knew we had struck upon a winning formula when the only complaint we got about the exercise was that we had left some people out of our feedback. We now keep a running list and coordinate among ourselves to make sure we mention every person in the group and try to keep frequency even and our comments truthful but constructive.

It's a simple enough technique to try with your own group, but it is vitally important that the people providing the critique are universally understood to be objective and skillful. Invite a couple of people you trust from outside the group to observe your debates, conversations, and behaviors. Then ask them for a brutally honest but well-intentioned critique of how the group behaves along the Right Fight Discipline Principles. Coaches, outside advisors, peers from other parts of the organization, and skillful organizational development professionals are all good sources to draw on in conducting this exercise.

ACKNOWLEDGMENTS

This book could not have been written without the contributions and encouragement of many people.

First and foremost, we would like to thank our many clients in companies across the globe and the extensive list of leaders who agreed to be interviewed for this book. Their insights, struggles, and leadership have taught and inspired us.

We are deeply grateful to Niko Canner, Jon Katzenbach, and the entire Katzenbach community for their belief in our work and their steadfast support of our efforts.

Special thanks to Nick Morgan for his commitment, wit, and extensive contributions—and to all the members of our team: including Nikki Smith-Morgan, Cindy Beyer, Alex Goldsmith, Corinne Lippie, Dee Dobbins, Tami Henderson, Matt Siegel, Todd Schuster, Esmond Harmsworth, Charles Sullivan, and Doug Reynolds.

Hollis Heimbouch, Matthew Inman, and many others at HarperCollins have been a wonderful team to work with. The book is better for their efforts and guidance.

Acknowledgments

Finally, for their love, encouragement, and patience as we devoted so much time and energy to this book, we would like to thank our families: Saj-nicole's parents Daniel and Thelma, and Kathy, Carol-Anne, Clifford, Darlene, Eric, Stephanie, Liz, and Alicia; Damon's parents June and Allen, and Anna, Drew, Tim, Elizabeth, Lisa, Zev, Bret, Erin, Pam, Bill R., Richard, Ginny, Simon, Solape, Paul, Karen, Bill B., Alex, and Patrick.

INDEX

ABOUT THE AUTHORS

SAJ-NICOLE JONI, PHD, is an internationally known business strategist and third-opinion advisor to senior executives and high-potential leaders. Engaging with Dr. Joni enables leaders to activate and sustain the full power of their capabilities to innovate, grow, execute, and drive performance. As a provocative and thoughtful sparring partner, she helps draw out leaders' best strategic thinking, viewing all sides of a problem, and testing multiple possibilities, even those at the boundaries of convention. Dr. Joni does not give advice; she gives leaders a way to frame the right questions and, through a robust vetting process, to uncover a richer, deeper set of answers and new questions.

Dr. Joni draws upon her senior leadership expertise as an executive at Microsoft and CSC Index, as well her extensive academic background, having served on the faculties of MIT, Carnegie Mellon University, and Wellesley College, to help leaders integrate across strategic, tactical, and political dimensions as well as across functional and business boundaries.

Her book *The Third Opinion: How Successful Leaders Use Outside Insight to Create Superior Results* (Portfolio, 2004) draws upon her long-established CEO advisory practice. A frequent speaker with a regular monthly column on Forbes.com, Dr. Joni has appeared on *Marketplace* on NPR and been published in *Harvard Business Review* and *Fast Company*. Dr. Joni is the founder and CEO of Cambridge International Group Ltd., and holds a PhD from the University of California, San Diego.

DAMON BEYER has been advising business leaders around the globe for over two decades. As a senior executive advisor at the firm of Booz & Company, and a founding member of the Katzenbach Center for Organizational Innovation, Beyer consults to senior executives in both the private and public sectors. He works with clients to create breakthrough organizational performance and unlock leadership potential buried deep within organizations. He draws on a broad range of strategic, operational, and organizational experience to help leaders unleash the full potential of their organizations. As a creative thinker, he helps frame new ways of thinking about old problems, breaking through conventional wisdom and generating new and practical insights. Often blending ideas from different industries, Beyer challenges his clients and teams to think big, value candor, and look for small things that can drive big results.

Beyer is currently helping to build Booz & Company's Texas and public sector practices and leads much of the firm's research on informal organization. Prior to joining Booz & Company, Beyer was a partner in the Texas office of Katzenbach Partners and McKinsey & Company, where he was a leader in the North American operations and global energy practices. Leadership development has always been a focus. While at McKinsey, Beyer redesigned and became the dean of McKinsey's most widely attended internal training program, the Introductory Leadership Workshop.

A frequent speaker on the subject of informal organization, Beyer has been published in *The McKinsey Quarterly, Harvard Business Review, BusinessFinance,* and *Oil & Gas Financial Journal.* Beyer earned a BS from the University of Louisiana and an MBA from Harvard Business School.